THE PENNY CAPITALISTS

Other books by John Benson:

Studies in the Yorkshire Coal Industry, Manchester 1976 (with R G Neville).

Rotherham As It Was, Nelson 1976 (with R G Neville).

Walsall As It Was, Nelson 1978 (with T J Raybould).

The West Riding: Unique Photographs of a Bygone Age, Clapham via Lancaster 1978.

British Coalminers in the Nineteenth Century: a Social History, Dublin 1980.

Bibliography of the British Coal Industry: Secondary Literature, Parliamentary and Departmental Papers, Mineral Maps and Plans and a Guide to Sources, Oxford 1981 (with R G Neville and C H Thompson).

JOHN BENSON

THE PENNY CAPITALISTS

A study of
Nineteenth-century
working-class Entrepreneurs

Rutgers University Press
New Brunswick, New Jersey

First published in the USA by
Rutgers University Press, 1983

Library of Congress Catalog Card No. 83-42695
ISBN 0-8135-1011-2

First published in Ireland by
Gill and Macmillan Ltd, 1983
© 1983 John Benson
All rights reserved
Printed in Great Britain

For Clare, Sally and Sophie

Contents

Acknowledgements

It is a pleasure to acknowledge the help which I have received in the preparation of this book. I am grateful to the many people who have provided me with ideas, advice and information: my colleagues Brenda Martin, Mike Boddington, Richard Hawkesworth, Mike Haynes, Geoff Hurd, Max Johnson and Jane Springett; Timothy Ashplant; Owen Ashton, North Staffordshire Polytechnic; Cyril Collard; Anne Digby, University of York; Peter Drake, Birmingham Reference Library; Edmund Frow; Dermot Healy, Manchester Polytechnic; Mike Jubb, Public Record Office; Joe Legatt; D.R. Mills, Open University; Doug Read, University of Hull; Gerry Rubin, University of Kent (who also commented most helpfully upon a first draft of the retailing section); John Saville, University of Hull; Alison M. Scott, University of Essex; Gareth Shaw, University of Exeter; Melanie Tebbutt, Manchester Polytechnic; and Michael Winstanley, University of Lancaster. I should also like to thank the Social Science Research Council for helping to finance the research, and The Polytechnic, Wolverhampton for allowing me both a period of study leave and the help of Jane Price in typing the final draft of the manuscript.

Parts of this study formed the basis of papers read to meetings of the Social History Society, the West Midland Group for the Study of Labour History and of the Sheffield City Polytechnic History Department Seminar; and the book as a whole has benefited from the comments and suggestions of those present. The book has benefited most, however, from the interest shown by those fellow historians who took time from their own work to read and comment upon an early version of my manuscript. Accordingly, my special thanks are due to my former colleague, George Bernard, now of the University of Southampton; to Ken Brown, of the Queen's University of Belfast; to Geoff Crossick, of the University of Essex; and to Elizabeth Roberts of the University of Lancaster. Without their perceptive advice this book would be much the poorer. Needless to say, any deficiencies which remain are my own responsibility.

Finally, and most importantly, my thanks are due to my wife, Clare, without whose encouragement the book would never have been started, let alone completed.

John Benson
Wolverhampton
December 1981

1

Introduction

I first became interested in penny capitalism while engaged in the research for a book on nineteenth-century coal-miners. Here was a group of workers about which I knew a good deal, a group about which I had completed my Ph.D. thesis, co-edited a book and written a dozen or more articles. Imagine my surprise when I came across several unpublished autobiographies at the Durham County Record Office in which miners described what was (to me at least) a completely new feature of coalfield life. It was with growing interest that I read of the many money-making activities undertaken by Durham miners and their families in the years before the First World War: they mended furniture and sharpened tools and cutlery, they made toffee and ginger beer, and on the coast they caught and sold fish. There seemed to exist a whole submerged economy about which I knew nothing and which had found no mention at all in the voluminous literature on nineteenth-century coal-mining communities. Further investigation among the available oral and autobiographical evidence soon confirmed that similar small-scale entrepreneurial activity had flourished in other coalfields too. All over the country miners and their wives seemed to be cutting hair, taking in washing and ironing, and turning their front rooms into little shops. I concluded, with some exaggeration perhaps, that in the coalfields 'Anybody with a marketable skill tried to turn it to good account.'[1]

Immediately two possibilities presented themselves. One was that this small-scale entrepreneurial activity was confined to the coalfields and so, though of some specialised interest, was unlikely to be of much concern to historians generally. The other — much more exciting — possibility was that this hidden form of enterprise had existed among working-class groups other than the miners to an extent which I, and apparently almost everybody else, had failed to realise. But if this small-scale entrepreneurial activity had indeed flourished among working people generally (and I soon discovered that it had), it was surely strange that it should have received so little attention. In fact, however, the neglect of what has been dubbed penny capitalism is not in the least surprising.

The first and fundamental reason for this neglect derives from the type of sources with which the would-be historian of penny capitalism has to deal. Indeed business archives generally pose serious difficulties for the unwary. Libraries and record offices abound with the records of the untypical: the large, progressive, successful enterprise on the one hand, the bankrupt failure on the other. The ordinary, run-of-the-mill concern is rarely to be found.[2] The problem is exacerbated in the case of penny capitalism. Few penny capitalists kept records; those that were kept rarely survive; and the handful which do survive are probably even more untypical than those rescued from larger business enterprises. Even the most scrupulous researcher may be seduced by the lack of evidence into believing either that penny capitalism did not exist or that, if it did exist, it was not very important.

This tendency has been reinforced by the second major reason for the neglect of penny capitalism: the prevailing attitudes and interests of those historians who might have been expected to investigate the hidden economy. In their different ways economic, business and labour historians have been concerned with size and success, concentration and consolidation — factors which for all their obvious importance serve only to accentuate still further the bias of the sources. Economic historians, it is fair to say, have tended to pay greatest attention to the most dynamic sectors of the economy, to stress the growing centralisation of production and labour in transport and the basic industries. The result has been that 'Any deviation from the factory system is usually treated as a historical footnote and explained away as an abnormality.'[3] Business historians, it is only too clear, have always been bewitched by success. Jonathan Boswell has put it well.

The picture has often been distorted. For one thing the writers have concentrated on the founders who were most successful, and particularly on those who initiated businesses which became really large and outstanding. The much larger category of middling founders and those who were less than brilliant, let alone the actual failures, have been ignored. Even within the category of the most successful, the literature may sometimes be biased, and a tendency to romanticize is common. It is to be expected that successful businessmen should sometimes indulge in ex-post facto rationalization, that official company histories should, with some outstanding exceptions, gild and burnish [or depreciate] their origins, and that older family firms should sentimentalize or venerate their founders.[4]

Nor have labour historians done enough to counteract the preoccupation of economic and business historicans with successful, capital-intensive, heavy industries such as coal-mining and iron-making for it was in this sector of the economy that industrial relations were most bitter and that the class struggle, it is argued, was being fought out. But this concentration on heavy industry is doubly unfortunate. In the first place, it diverts attention from the very sector of the economy — that concerned with services — in which, it will be seen later, penny capitalism was best able to flourish. In the second place, the preoccupation with heavy industry has encouraged labour historians to concentrate upon organised, collective (particularly trade union) efforts at working-class self-improvement. But trade union histories, whatever their other merits, cannot be expected to explore fully the non-institutional features of working-class life. Indeed by presenting a view of working people at home and at work which appears to be both consistent and convincing, they may actually retard our understanding of an informal, small-scale, and often part-time activity such as penny capitalism.[5]

For economic, business and labour historians alike penny capitalism has remained on the margins: at best unimportant, at worst unknown. It is only very recently, for example, that historians have begun to show any understanding of the complex ways by which nineteenth and early twentieth-century working people actually made their living. It is clear already, however, that few families were dependent simply upon a single, regular, weekly wage. Much employment was seasonal or casual in nature and most families derived their income from a whole cluster of different sources: from work done by the wife and children, from begging, from the Poor Law, and from petty crime such as coal picking or poaching.[6] It is from this new understanding of working-class incomes that a handful of historians have started to examine submerged activities such as penny capitalism. Two contributions stand out. In a vivid essay published in 1975 Raphael Samuel demonstrated the enormous importance of petty entrepreneurial activity to the inhabitants of Headington Quarry on the outskirts of Oxford. Two years later, in a study of working-class standards of living in Lancaster and Barrow-in-Furness, Elizabeth Roberts confronted the 'apparent paradox of a healthier-than-average population existing on earnings near or below the poverty line'. Part of the explanation, she discovered, lay in the various types of small-scale enterprise being undertaken by working people in these towns.[7] Neither writer would claim, I am sure, to have touched upon more than a few aspects of working-class entrepreneurial activity; but their lead, their insights and their use of evidence have encouraged me to undertake the detailed study of nineteenth-century penny capitalism which forms the subject of this book.

Unfortunately, however, it is no easy task to find even a working definition of penny capitalism. The term, which was first coined by the anthropologist Sol Tax in 1953, has never been clearly defined.[8] Nor is it easy to do so. Indeed it is conceptually and historically impossible to distinguish clearly penny capitalists from wage-labourers below and from the petty bourgeoisie above. Subsequent chapters will show, for example, how working people became penny capitalists for short periods or on a part-time basis. Nor is this just the easy evasion of a historian in difficulties, for it will be a basic contention of the book that the very difficulty of defining penny capitalism is fundamental to an understanding of it.

Nonetheless a definition is certainly needed. Perhaps the most fruitful approach is to begin by excluding three groups which might appear at first glance to be penny capitalists. Neither outworkers, nor the self-employed (who hired out their own labour), nor sub-contractors (who hired out the labour of others) were penny capitalists. Even if they were responsible for the provision of working capital, 'the mere ownership of tools does not make the weaver an "independent manufacturer", any more than it does the farm labourer who owns a spade an independent farmer.'[9] All three groups still lacked one essential characteristic of any capitalist endeavour: that the capitalist should maintain control over the use to which his capital and labour was put. This then was the first defining characteristic of the penny capitalist, that he (or she) should be responsible for the whole process, however small: from acquiring the necessary capital, choosing a site, bargaining for raw materials, deciding the working methods, and providing the tools, to finding a market for the finished product.[10]

This independence leads directly to the second defining characteristic of the penny capitalist: that, like the capitalist proper, he was prepared to assume risks in the hope of making profits. It was this speculative element which again set the penny capitalist apart from the outworker, the self-employed workman and the sub-contractor. The third characteristic of the penny capitalist was that he should be of working-class origin. In theory, of course, such a prescription can give rise to as many difficulties as it resolves; but in practice it will be seen to pose relatively few difficulties. Fourth, and vaguest of all, the penny capitalist needed to operate on a small scale. It is impossible to define precisely the maximum size which a penny capitalist's business could attain without breaching the bounds of penny capitalism. But his capital, his turnover and his profits should all be measured, if not in pennies, then in pounds and shillings rather than in hundreds, thousands or tens of thousands of pounds.

In principle, then, this set of four criteria makes it easy to recognise the nineteenth and early twentieth-century penny capitalist. The practice, naturally, is rather less straightforward for, as with any social group, those on the margins are harder to identify than those at the centre. Thus the coalminer selling beer from his front room in the evenings was clearly a penny capitalist; but what of the foreman who gave up a factory job to run his own pawnshop? What of the artisan proprietor of a

small gun firm which made parts for larger concerns? Nonetheless, it remains possible to define the penny capitalist as a
working man or woman who went into business on a small
scale in the hope of profit (but with the possibility of loss)
and made him (or her) self responsible for every facet of the
enterprise.

The purpose of this book is to explore this still almost
totally neglected subject of penny capitalism. More specifically, it is intended to pursue three broad lines of inquiry.
Attention will be directed in the first place towards simply
rescuing penny capitalism from obscurity; towards discovering the forms which it assumed, the kinds of local economy
which sustained it, the ways in which it was conducted, the
amount of employment it provided, the types of people whom
it attracted, and the success (or otherwise) with which it was
carried out. The second major line of inquiry will involve a
reconsideration of the generally accepted view (assumption
might be a better word) that small, self-employed producers
of all kinds were seriously threatened by the centripetal
force of urban industrial development. By the end of the century, it is said, their local monopolies had been destroyed by
better transport and new methods of marketing and they were
being 'squeezed by the concentration of capital, the advance
of large-scale production, and the rise of cartels and monopolies'.[11] Such views will be challenged most strongly. It will
be suggested in fact that 'The small-scale and labour intensive
sector was not a survival, but a central and dynamic component of mid [and late] – Victorian growth.'[12] The third
major line of inquiry will involve an examination of the
impact which penny capitalism had upon some of the most
important issues currently under discussion in the field of
labour and social history: the role of the working-class family
(and particularly of its female members); the extent to which,
as is generally assumed, 'working people were slowly but
assuredly being moulded into a homogeneous working class
which enjoyed a common work experience and outlook';[13]
the degree of economic and social mobility out of the working class; and finally, the impact which penny capitalism had
upon working class political and labour organisation.

These are important questions. It is hoped therefore that

this study will prove of interest not just to specialists, but to all those concerned with the history of British society during the nineteenth and early twentieth centuries.

2

Mining and Fishing

The primary industries of mining, fishing and farming offered varied scope for penny capitalist enterprise. Of the three, mining provided working people with the fewest opportunities to turn their work skills to their own account; for to compete successfully in any branch of extractive industry the aspiring entrepreneur needed not only considerable amounts of capital and of credit but also technical expertise and specialised marketing skills — a combination formidable enough to deter all but the most exceptional working man.

Yet penny capitalism did survive in tiny, scattered enclaves. Sand was dredged from the River Thames, gravel quarried from 'big grubbing holes' near Canterbury, and jet dug at Whitby on the east coast of Yorkshire by quasi-independent miners who rented patches of ground and sold their output to local manufacturers. Demand was stimulated both by royal patronage and by the Great Exhibition of 1851 so that by 1864 some 250 petty entrepreneurs made their living by digging the jet.[1] There were also opportunities in the more substantial salt trade of Worcestershire and Cheshire: 'it is to the credit of the watermen on the Weaver', it was said in 1915,

> that they consisted largely of careful men, and accumulated money. It is very doubtful whether on any navigation in the kingdom so fine a body of watermen, or one so careful and striving, ever existed. As soon as a waterman by carefulness has accumulated a little money, if he was a pushing man, he took a little set of works of two or three pans and made salt enough to keep his flat working steadily.[2]

Small-scale capitalistic enterprise lingered too in the lead mining districts of Cumberland, Derbyshire, north Yorkshire and North Wales. Until the end of the eighteenth century it was common for mining partnerships to include one or two men who had risen from the ranks and were made responsible for day-to-day management. Some partnerships, like that running the Lane End mine in Swaledale in 1801, were even dominated by working miners. But in north Yorkshire these small adventurers were soon displaced by their inability to meet the growing capital requirements of deeper and more sophisticated mining, a process hastened still further by the depressions of 1815 and 1829–33. However these 'Poor Men's Ventures' survived rather longer in Derbyshire and in Cumberland where even the mid-nineteenth-century dominance of a firm like the London Lead Company at Alston Moor did not prevent 'a very great number of cases in which poor men, having little or no capital, but depending chiefly on their labour, get two or three partners with a little money, perhaps, to assist them, and they continue the trials in that manner'. Indeed as late as 1876 it could be said of lead mining in Derbyshire that 'With a few exceptions . . . the mining of the present day . . . is limited to "poor men's mines", or small adventures, in which with none but the simplest mechanical aid old works are explored again which scarcely invited the attention of a company'.[3]

The possibilities open to the few workers in jet, salt and lead mining pale almost into insignificance when compared to the lack of entrepreneurial opportunities available to the huge, and ever increasing, number of workers employed in the coal-mining industry. Yet even here every strike and lock-out did see an outburst of primitive mining in the form of outcropping and picking from the spoil heaps, usually for domestic consumption but sometimes for sale. There were many stratagems. Thus during the course of a strike at Pendleton, Lancashire in 1911 the men used to break up bricks 'and they'd put pitch on them or blacklead them, put them in a bag put good coal on top and sell them to the people in Clairemont Road and district for 1s. 6d. a bag. The people that had the money . . .'[4] In later disputes outcropping became a highly organised business with men, women and children working in shifts, each keeping to their own 'stall'. 'One would not say anything about them fetching a bag or a barrowful for their own use,' explained the vice-president of the Derbyshire Miners' Association during the 1921 lock-out, 'but when it comes to sending hundreds of tons away, there is the evil. My contention is that had any of them attempted to do such a thing prior to the lock-out they would have been prosecuted for stealing coal.'[5]

Some coal-miners went into production on a slightly more permanent, though still chronically insecure, basis. Thus the mining booms of the 1870s and the 1890s both saw small pits being opened (or reopened) in Warwickshire. In 1890–91 a Bedworth miner, William Dennis, sunk two shafts to a maximum depth of thirty four yards, just a few feet from the Coventry-Nuneaton railway line, and sold his coal from the pithead. This, however, was the exception which proved the rule. By the 1840s the Forest of Dean 'free miners' with their 'small scale proprietorship of the land and the coal', had been reduced to the level of wage-earners and by 1850 it cost getting on for £3,000 to sink a pit even to the accessible Thick Coal that lay beneath the Black Country. Thus the working out of the shallowest seams and the growing sophistication of the industry meant that by the middle of the century there was virtually no opportunity for coal-miners even to enter junior management, let alone to join the ranks of their employers. So despite the survival of penny capitalism in some of its minor branches, the mining industry as a whole was becoming too complex and capital-intensive to enable it to satisfy the entrepreneurial aspirations of ambitious working men.[6]

Thus in the primary sector penny capitalist energy tended to be directed towards fishing and farming, pursuits which like building and handicrafts underwent very little technical change as a result of industrialisation. Fishing depended of course upon the accessibility of suitable, well-stocked water; but wherever this was available there was sure to be some kind of fishing, with part at least of the catch being put up for sale. The simplest and cheapest way to start fishing on a commercial basis was to obtain a rod and line, a few lobster pots, or some type of fixed net which could be operated from the shore. The use of such fixed or 'kettle' nets was common around Dungeness on the south-eastern tip of Kent. A Lydd man remembers that his father had worked on somebody else's nets in the mid-nineteenth century but was then given a net stand and licence by his brother so that he could begin to work for himself. The nets were put down in the spring in the hope of catching herring, corbeam, sole and in particular mackerel. Fixed-net fishing was not without its difficulties. Sometimes boats ran into the nets; sometimes the weather changed for the worse before there was time to get the nets in ('We've had them tore all to pieces'); and sometimes there were unwelcome visitors:

> there was only two of you. You got a lot of fish you've got a job on the sands, you take them up and shoot them down, they'll [gypsies] be up there pinching them. And they'll look all round when you'd pulled them all in, if they see a nice salmon they'd stick that down their jumper.[7]

Although never more than a part-time job, kettle-netting was always undertaken on a serious, commercial basis. Nor was this form of fishing unimportant in the local economy. It provided a welcome, supplementary source of income in an area where full-time jobs were not always easy to find and accounted, indeed, for half the mackerel landed at Dungeness, one of the top eight or nine mackerel fishing stations in the country.[8]

For the man with ambition, however, starting to fish generally meant wanting to acquire a boat of his own. Nor was this an impossible dream in the early years of the nineteenth century, when the typical trawling smack was skippered by its owner and crewed by his neighbours and relations. In fact as late as 1882 most of the men owning more than one boat in the deep-sea ports of Hull and Grimsby were said to have begun their careers as apprentices. Such upward economic mobility became decidedly more difficult with the industrialisation of the east coast fishing industry. Vessels built after 1880 were fitted with steam capstans to haul in their nets and by the end of the century the deep-sea ships themselves were predominantly steam driven. 'Steam vessels', it has been said, 'expensive to build, maintain and run, certainly put a final stop to the ownership aspirations of working fishermen'.[9]

Yet it would be a mistake to assume that the introduction of steam power to deep-sea fishing meant the disappearance of penny capitalist opportunity from the whole of the industry. This was very far from the case. Communities reacted differently to changes in fishing technology. Inshore fishing remained very much the province of the small man, for there were all sorts of ways of gaining access to a rowing boat or a small sailing ship. Loans could be arranged or friends and relatives prevailed upon. A boy brought up in Barrow-in-Furness remembers that when his father was not labouring at the steel-works, he used to go out in a boat belonging to an uncle who lived with the family. Nor did a formal share in the ownership of a boat have to be very expensive: when a small partnership based at Portlethen near Aberdeen broke up in 1877, one of the partners claimed only three pounds as his share of the vessel. Informal family partnerships were probably the most common way of raising capital. Two late-nineteenth-century examples from opposite ends of England will illustrate the point. On the Cumberland coast 'the men of Flimby were great fishermen . . . several families had combined their savings to buy a boat of their own, and there were quite a number of these.' Meanwhile at Dengemarsh in Kent a farm worker went into partnership with his brother in the mid 1870s. 'They bought an old boat I think, then after a while got one a little better and such like.'[10]

Easy as it is to discover scattered references to working-class participation in commercial fishing, it is far harder to judge the importance of this involvement and to determine whether or not it declined with the industrialisation of the industry. It is quite clear however that penny capitalist fishing had not been destroyed by the end of the century. Although there is no way of assessing the (obviously large) number of workers who went fishing in their spare time, it is possible to attempt some estimate of the contribution made by full (or nearly full) time penny capitalists to the late-nineteenth and early-twentieth-century fishing industry. From 1891 onwards the census authorities attempted to distinguish in certain occupations between employers, employees and those working on their own account. Fishing was one of these occupations; and although the returns generally were described as 'excessively untrustworthy', they do allow a tentative generalisation to be made. They show that even after 1891 more than a quarter of all the men employed in the fishing industry of England and Wales claimed to be self-employed, and of these a high proportion must surely have been working class.[11]

These penny capitalist fishermen worked hard to protect their investment. Boats and tackle had to be kept in good condition. Nets were mended in winter when fishing was impossible and, according to some, boats had to be scrubbed every two weeks throughout the year because they became 'almost roughcasted in a fortnight'.[12] Although these inshore fishermen rarely ventured more than six or seven miles out to sea and usually returned to land within the day, it took a good deal of skill and experience to find, never mind to catch, the fish: 'Hadn't got like they have now, echo sounders and fish finders and all that . . . well of course, before the first war it was all sailing, see you had to work with the tides a lot.'[13] The fishermen had to be prepared to switch from one type of catch to another. On the Colne and Blackwater estuaries in Essex it was roker and dab in the autumn, sprat and shellfish in the winter, and roker and sole in the spring. Off the south-east coast of Kent it used to be herring from late October until Christmas; sprat from November till February; and mackerel from the start of May to the end of July and again from the beginning of September until the middle of October.[14]

As soon as the penny capitalist was catching fish in any quantity, he had to devote some thought to their disposal. There were various possibilities, each with its own advantage and its particular drawbacks. The simplest method was to sell the fish to whatever wholesalers or members of the public happened to be waiting when the boat docked. This method of distribution, though convenient, was unlikely of course to secure the highest prices. More profitable, perhaps, but certainly more time-consuming, was for members of the family to hawk the catch around the streets, sell it to the local fishmonger, or take it to the nearest town.[15] The coming of the railways made it possible for even small fishermen to serve new markets further afield. In the south of England the full cost of carriage to Billingsgate came to be paid by the wholesaler but, recalls one fisherman, you had to be trusting because you only received a cheque for the amount which he decided to send you. For the small fisherman without a bank account, there was the additional problem of cashing the cheque, either with a nearby grocer or with the very local wholesaler to whom the fish might have been sold in the first place. There was one other possibility. In parts of south-east Kent it was the custom in the winter for some boats to sell all their mackerel to a canning factory at Deal. There was never much bargaining, explained one fisherman, because the firm paid 6s. 6d., carriage found: 'It saved a lot of trouble you see.'[16] Despite the growing range of outlets for their catches, most penny capitalists, like other fishermen, switched from one to another as seemed most convenient. Thus in the summer of 1883 fishermen at Newlyn, just outside Penzance, began to sell their mackerel to local hawkers because they were too small to send further afield.[17]

The profits from fishing were almost always divided between skipper and crew according to a system of shares. In late-nineteenth-century Kent and Essex, for example, the owner of a three man vessel would receive sixty per cent of the profits, with the other forty per cent being shared by the two crew.[18] Unfortunately, however, it is almost impossible to determine the actual amount of profit to be shared out in this way. In the first place, it is doubtful whether these small, self-employed fishermen, any more than other penny capi-talists, ever kept reliable financial records; almost certainly none survive. In the second place, fishing was always a pre-carious occupation. There was the interference from other boats, the unpredictability of the fish, and the constant threat from bad weather. Every penny capitalist's investment, whether it be a lobster pot or a sailing boat, was at perpetual risk. In 1879 two working fishermen from near Penzance bought a pilchard-boat, the *Try*, for £110; they failed to pay the insurance on her and were 'simply ruined' when the boat was wrecked in 1883.[19] And although in winter some owners were able to hire out their craft or engage in salvage, most could do little to counteract the sharp drop in income which occurred at the end of every summer season. Thus a Whit-stable man remembers that while his father sometimes made as much as a shilling a pound on Dover sole during the summer months, he was happy if he was able to average a pound a week profit throughout the entire year. Inshore fishing did offer interest, independence, an outdoor life and, in summer at least, a reasonable income. Harry Matthews remembers that in his boyhood Faversham oyster dredgers were reckoned better off than the local brickmakers who had to work a five or six day week. After all, he points out, the dredgers used to pay a pub landlord five shillings just to let them count their oysters on his verandah.[20]

However much better off some full-time, penny capitalist fishermen were than their neighbours in other jobs, they did not regard boat ownership as a means of social advance.

> Fishing communities where the share system operated were almost classless. There was no antagonism between the boat owner and his crew: their interests were identical. Threats to their welfare came not from internal disagreements but from the activities of rival groups or outsiders like the middlemen to whom they frequently sold their catch. Since the boats which they used were still relatively small, it was feasible for every crew member, given reasonable luck and a degree of thrift, that all-important Victorian virtue, to aspire to own his own boat. Similarly a run of poor seasons, or the loss of his uninsured boat, could quickly reduce a boat owner to a simple fisherman again. This state of affairs, involving a host of vulnerable entrepreneurs who required a low capital outlay and who not only worked in conjunction with a small group of other men but shared the profits with them, differed immeasurably from the system operated in farming and most manufacturing industry. It engendered cooperation rather than fostering class antagonism.[21]

Like coal-miners, fishermen and their families found it difficult to escape from their class background. When the wife of a fisherman living in Aqueduct Street, Preston left him in the early years of this century, he put out a big notice: 'half a bed to let'.[22]

Although penny capitalist fishing offered few opportunities for upward social mobility, this does not detract from its importance in coastal communities. Part-time fishing enabled many workmen to supplement inadequate and irregular family incomes. Moreover the increasing capitalisation of the deep-sea industry created new possibilities: it encouraged some families to raise the money needed to enable them to rely upon inshore fishing as their chief means of support.

3

Farming

Important though fishing remained, of the three primary industries it was farming which allowed penny capitalists to make their greatest contribution towards expanding the productive capacity of the country. Nor is it surprising that the nineteenth century should see a surge of working-class interest in keeping animals and growing vegetables and flowers. Gardening or tending an allotment offered the growing number of town and city dwellers a hobby that was in complete contrast to their everyday work. Moreover, in both town and country it provided a refuge from the wife and children and held out pleasant, if often illusory, prospects of fresh food or even of 'a stage towards and an education for the taking of a small holding'.[1]

Not least among the attractions of gardening and allotment holding was the low cost of starting. For those with a garden of their own it cost next to nothing. Even those without land could occasionally sidestep any initial capital outlay. In parts of the Scottish lowlands, for example, it was the custom for shepherds to be allowed to keep a cow and to run a flock of sheep along with their employers' stock. In open villages, like Headington Quarry on the outskirts of Oxford, the notorious 'rolling fence' had sometimes brought land ownership within almost universal reach: 'up went the fence, that was theirs'.[2] Some employers made land available: a Faversham brickworker remembers that, at the end of the century, 'Pretty nigh every man, if he was a moulder or bearer or temperer in the brickfields, you got a bit of allotment for nothing, they give you a bit of ground.'[3] Even when the full market price had to be paid, this was unlikely to be prohibitively expensive. Thus at the beginning of the present century (when, for instance, Nottinghamshire farmworkers were earning a pound a week and Cumberland coal-face workers about twice this sum), allotments all over the country were being let for between 2*s*. 6*d*. and 10*s*. a year. Sometimes, too, it was possible to buy an allotment on credit: in Northamptonshire many members of the Desborough Co-operative Society were said to 'pay for their plots out-right, otherwise payment is made by instalments. A very common way is for a member to leave the annual amount of profit credited to him towards liquidating the cost of purchase; in this way he buys the land almost without knowing it.'[4]

If the cost of acquiring land could often be kept down, so too could that of stocking it. Flower and vegetable seeds posed no great difficulty. A Lancaster man remembers that his family used to buy a 'penny packet of seeds or ha'penny, whatever they may be. A packet of lettuce seeds cost a ha'penny.'[5] Meanwhile, near Oxford, 'These old chaps never reckoned to buy seed potatoes – they used to swap with someone else . . . make a change . . . he'd save some seed out of his and I'd save seed, and then we'd change them over. Perhaps he had a bit of ground that was heavy, and you had some ground that was light . . .'[6] Fertiliser too could be obtained fairly easily. Fallen oak and beech leaves, urged the *Smallholder*, should be turned into valuable leaf-mould. For those with strong stomachs there was manure in abundance even in the towns: 'horses used to do it in the street you see, and people used to go out and get it in their buckets from the street.'[7] The son of a Lancashire railway labourer remembers that around the turn of the century,

> We used to go following the horses for manure for the garden. There was a chap had a confectioners and sweet stall and he had a little pony and trap and dad . . . cleared it out twice a week with a great big barrow that dad made and we used to go and load this manure up, then take it from Paxton Terrace down to the garden. We used to do that twice a week.[8]

It was much more difficult to raise the money needed to start rearing livestock. All that the *Smallholder* could suggest, for example, was that it might sometimes be possible to obtain a swarm of bees for nothing. But there is no doubt that if the gardener or allotment holder could somehow raise the money needed to buy animals, by joining a pig club perhaps, he would probably be able to feed them fairly cheaply. In the country-side, goats, rabbits, pigs and poultry could be fed largely with food stolen from the farms, with wild flowers and plants, or with harvest gleanings and acorns — commonly known as 'pig-nuts'. It was said that after the corn had been harvested in Lincolnshire, 'most of women and children came to glean from the stubble. In the normal way they would get sufficient to feed the family pig during the winter.'[9] In urban areas it was sometimes possible to obtain animal feed on credit, but everywhere it was household waste which provided the staple food of the family pig. 'Mother bought two little pigs . . . and mother used to go down of a morning and I used to go down with her with the pig swill, whatever one had left and bread, boil all the potato peelings, cabbage peelings, everything went in for the pigs.'[10]

Informed contemporary interest in all aspects of the land question makes it easier to measure working-class participa-tion in gardening and allotment holding than in almost any other form of penny capitalist activity. Naturally enough most observers stressed the rural nature of allotment holding. Cer-tainly in the early years of the nineteenth century allotments, like gardens, were most common in the countryside, par-ticularly in the Midlands and south of England where agricul-tural wages were at their lowest. It was estimated in 1833, for example, that while forty two per cent of all parishes in England and Wales contained quarter to half acre allotments, the proportion varied from as low as twelve per cent of parishes in Yorkshire to as high as eighty two per cent of those in Wiltshire. The number of rural allotments increased significantly during the final quarter of the century so that by 1886 nearly ninety per cent of the country's 900,000 farm servants, cottagers and agricultural labourers were said to have the use of a garden or allotment of at least an eighth of an acre.[11]

It would be a serious mistake to assume, however, that gar-dening and allotment holding became exclusively — or even predominantly — a rural activity.[12] Better off working men continued to rent allotments in urban areas throughout the country: in towns and cities as varied as, for example, Barrow-in-Furness, Birmingham, Coventry, Desborough, London, Northampton, Nottingham, Oxford, Saffron Walden, Saltaire, Sheffield, Southampton, Waltham Forest, Wellingborough and York. While it is true that with time there came a decline in the amount of urban land available for use as allotments, the number of individual plots actually increased. Thus oral investigation shows that in turn of the century Barrow and Preston a third, and in Lancaster a half, of all respondents' fathers kept allotments. So although they were presumably less common in larger towns and cities, there were still in 1914 some 325,000 urban allotments in England and Wales, a third more than in the countryside, even if they were on average only a third as large.[13]

Of course it is impossible to assume that every garden and allotment in the country was worked solely — or even chiefly — with an eye to the market. Not infrequently allotment tenancy agreements specifically forbade sales from being made. Even when production was essentially for family consumption, it was but a short step to producing for sale. In fact it was probably difficult to avoid entering the market at some level: 'If you'd got a lot of fowl, anybody 'ud come to your house, and ask if you'd got half a dozen eggs, they used to get rid of the surplus like that, they didn't do it as a business, but . . . anybody want half a dozen eggs they'd come to you for 'em.'[14] Sometimes the difficulty of distinguishing production for domestic consumption from production for the local market is reflected in the confusion of the surviving oral testimony. The son of a Lancashire railway labourer recalls how his parents tended their garden and kept hens in the backyard: 'It was just for the family', he explains, 'Mother used to sell odds and ends like lettuce.'[15] It seems that the majority of small producers probably did add to their earnings by selling their stock and produce. Some families sold half their pig to pay off their debts, while others were able to keep two pigs — one for consumption and one for sale. Indeed some gardeners and allotment holders proved as strongly profit motivated as the most devoted capitalist could wish. A seventeen-year-old factory worker wrote proudly to the *Smallholder* in 1910 to announce that he was able to sell most of his produce to his mother. 'Thus we follow out the principle in practice of producing at home instead of buying from the "foreigner".'[16] A girl from Barrow-in-Furness remembers with more bitterness that during the same period her step-grandfather 'had a garden on Greengate where the nursery school is now and he used to bring all the vegetables, potatoes, cabbage, beans and the most beautiful tomatoes anybody had ever tasted and believe it or not he used to charge my mother for it'.[17]

In assessing the prevalence of agricultural penny capitalism the difficulty then is to establish not only the number of gardens and allotments that were run by working families, but also the extent of their often casual and informal production for the market. These difficulties are not easily solved. The evidence does suggest, however, that nearly all the 670,000 allotments in England and Wales in 1914 were run by working people who, at one time or another, tried to sell part of their produce. At the most conservative estimate, therefore, there were well over half a million working-class families in Great Britain (one in ten of the total) trying to make money from their gardens and allotments at the beginning of this century.

The chief resource of these gardeners and allotment holders, as of all penny capitalists, was their labour, not their capital. Accordingly the land was worked as intensively, and with as much individual care, as was possible. Country women sometimes helped to grow flowers and vegetables. Here is one Norfolk girl's account of how her mother made their garden pay:

My Dad worked in a railway works two miles away, and we had one acre of garden so that he and my Mother spent every spare minute working in it. She planted all the seeds and managed the cucumber frames. I remember that one rather poor and large family always sent on Sundays for a halfpenny cucumber, which Mother interpreted as all the curly mis-shapen ones. The garden provided us with fruit and vegetables but my Mother also sold fruit and flowers to supplement the family income, and many were the young men who came on Sunday morning for a buttonhole, a favourite being a bud of the 'Gloire de Dijon' which grew on the wall.[18]

More often it was the man who saw to the garden, and certainly the allotment was very much a male preserve. Many men put in an hour or two before and/or after their normal day's work, calling on the rest of the family to help when necessary. An Oxford man remembers potato-pulling best. 'The old man used to march us up there. I can hear him now, when we were picking up 'taters. "Take 'em up, don't tread the buggers in."'[19] The land could soon become an obsession: a workman at the Great Western Railway works in Swindon pointed out that,

> Very often the village resident will work for an hour in his garden or attend to his pigs and domestic animals before leaving for the railway shed . . . Paul's home is in the village, about three miles from the town. There he passes his leisure in comparative quiet, and in his spare time from the shed, cultivates a large plot of land and keeps pigs . . . He takes great interest in his roots and crops, and almost worships his forty perch of garden.[20]

The penny capitalist could afford to keep animals only if they were cheap to buy and feed, yielded a reasonably quick profit, and responded well to the personal care and attention which was the small producer's only advantage over his larger competitors. Some families went in for breeding rabbits, cage birds or dogs, and many more kept chickens.[21] But it was the pig which was the mainstay of the small allotment. Not only were pigs easy to feed, but they matured quickly: 'It all works in together, the pigs keep the groun' in good 'eart, and the groun' grows the pig-food.'[22] Accordingly pigs were everywhere. Of the 2,193 working-class families living in West Bromwich in 1837, 192 were said to keep pigs. A few years later the Notting Hill district of London housed about a thousand people, most of whom made their living by rearing and fattening pigs. The owners collected kitchen refuse from nearby middle and upper-class homes, fed it to the pigs, whose meat they sold in turn to the very people from whom they had collected their feed — a classic economic and environmental 'cycle of mutual benefit'.[23] Although late-nineteenth- and early-twentieth-century sanitary legislation made it increasingly difficult to keep pigs in built-up areas, it seems hardly to have affected their popularity in either small towns or the countryside. At the turn of the century Barrow-in-Furness ironworkers had 'a lot of what they called the gardens. They weren't gardens, there were a number of old sheds and shanties where they kept hens and pigs. Quite a few people had pigs. You could hear them squealing and doing when they killed them.'[24] Here a Lincolnshire man recalls the continuing importance of the family pig in the decades before the First World War.

Every cottage labourer had one pig or more. They were his most important possessions ... pigs were always a big topic of conversation in the village, and after the usual greeting it was quite normal to ask how the pigs were doing ...

After a pig in the district had been killed the important thing was to buy one to feed for next year, and there was much talk and speculation when a sow had farrowed a litter. The piglets would be furtively looked at during the first few weeks after birth, for they were not marketable until they were eight weeks old. By this time, if the litter was any good, the pigs were spoken for by one or another ...

The most important club in the village was the Pig Club, and my father was its secretary for more than thirty years. The subscription was 6*d.* a month per pig. In the case of illness the secretary was immediately notified, and a committee of inspection was sent. They would decide if the pig had to be destroyed and whether anything could be salvaged. On an average, not more than one or two died in a year, and we never had a major catastrophe like foot-and-mouth disease, which would have swamped the funds. After fifty years the Club had accumulated £90. It gave an annual supper except when there had been an extra drain on the funds. This was the big social event at the inn, and everybody would go through his own particular repertory of songs. There were four courses to the meal; beef, mutton, pork and plum pudding. The hearty eaters sampled each dish in turn, to see which they liked best. Having decided this, they would really settle down to it. I had my first half-pint of beer at one of these suppers, but the normal helping was a quart.[25]

Despite — or perhaps because of — the care which these part-time penny capitalists lavished upon their crops and livestock, they tended to pay relatively little attention to marketing. This is most important for it meant that as in fishing, wives and children were allowed to help with the selling; and the children's participation means in turn that marketing is the aspect of gardening and allotment holding about which oral investigation has been able to reveal most. Oral evidence confirms indeed that some small producers were not very strongly profit motivated. You had to look after your friends and neighbours, and particularly your relatives: 'if you'd an allotment', recalls a Lancaster man, 'all your friends would come round of a Sunday morning and admire all that you'd got and there was a little bit of quiet cadging. There was quite a lot given away.'[26]

It has been seen, however, that other small producers were strongly profit motivated and that most did sell at least part of their surplus. It was simplest and cheapest to let would-be purchasers come to the garden or allotment: 'Mother used to sell stuff from the door. Somebody would come for a penny-worth of lettuce . . . The new potatoes she used to sell a few of those outside'.[27] The *Smallholder* had more ambitious plans.

> A swinging ornamental sign should be fixed up over the garden gate, informing passers-by that fresh flowers are obtainable, the parlour window should be suitably 'dressed', and a slanting green baize-covered board, or a glass case which any handy carpenter could manufacture, be mounted on a pillar by the fence, to hold buttonholes and bodice sprays. These find ready purchasers.[28]

Few gardeners or allotment holders went to these lengths. For whatever the trappings, selling from home had obvious limitations; so it was always tempting for the small producer to take the marketing initiative by sending his children out round the immediate neighbourhood. They soon learned how best to dispose of their meat, skins, milk, eggs, flowers, vegetables and other produce. The son of a Lancaster mill fireman remembers that from about 1907 onwards,

Father used to grow lettuce and he had a small greenhouse and he used to grow tomatoes. I used to sell them. I used to go out with a basket or a bogie, a little box of wheels, and I used to go to the better class houses on Freehold, Derwent Road. I had my customers every week — 'Come again next Saturday morning.' Lettuce were twopence and threepence, great big lovely lettuce.[29]

Otherwise, rabbit skins continued to be sold to rag and bone men and other produce taken to local fruiterers, greengrocers and pork dealers or sold in the nearest market. In Worcestershire 'A great number of the small people or their wives . . . are dealers and higglers. A woman will take 500 eggs to Kidderminster on a market-day, of which perhaps 50 would be her own, and the rest her neighbours', for whom she sells on a small commission.'[30] There was little change then in the time-honoured ways by which working people disposed of the produce from their gardens and allotments. Even more than in fishing, selling remained what it had always been: simple, local and strongly personal. There is no sign here of the increasingly sophisticated marketing techniques being adopted in other sectors of the economy. Nor, despite the use made of local shopkeepers, is there any real indication of a growing separation between the productive and distributive functions.

However working people chose to dispose of their produce, it is of course extremely difficult to estimate the profits or losses which they made from their gardens and allotments. In fact, the lack of direct evidence, common to so much penny capitalistic activity, is aggravated rather than eased by the arguments of contemporary enthusiasts, all of whom tended to overestimate the benefits to be derived from any access to the land. It was maintained in 1843, for example, that it was possible for a worker to make four pounds a year from a quarter of an acre of land. Forty years later J L Green concluded that:

As to the monetary returns from the cultivation of allotments, we may quote the following instance (one of many to the same effect), the particulars of which were supplied to us by the occupier himself. He said that after paying for a considerable portion of the labour incidental to a plot of twenty-six perches, he found, at the end of the season, that his 'returns' covered all expenses, rent included, leaving a balance of four sacks of potatoes, and sufficient green-stuff to last through the winter; and this, taking no account of the produce consumed by his household during the whole of the summer. There could, he said, be no room for the question, 'Will it pay?' And he went on to observe: 'The truth is, and I do not exaggerate in asserting it, that it can be made to pay fifty per cent; and those, therefore, who invest in the Savings Bank, at three per cent, or less, and could manage an allotment, had better re-consider their policy.'[31]

Despite such claims, it is clear that all sorts of difficulties could and often did arise. It was not always possible to get an allotment of suitable size. It was found in Oxfordshire, at least, that the one acre allotment was both too large and too small: too large for the man regularly employed as a farm labourer, too small for the man aspiring to independence. Moreover the land might be of poor quality or situated a long way from the tenant's home. Not that proximity alone was any guarantee of success or security: when road building was undertaken in Barrow-in-Furness in the decade before the First World War it destroyed many allotments. 'Central Drive was pegged through and they gave my father notice to quit, that they were going to build a road and before he'd got all his stuff off, the pegs were in the garden where Central Drive was coming.'[32] Even a conveniently located plot of suit-able size could pose difficulties. The tenancy might be hedged about with restrictions, forbidding the keeping of pigs, for example, in case pig food was stolen from local farms. Then there was always the weather to contend with. Alexander Somerville's dreams were shattered by Scotland's dry summer of 1826.

During March and April of that year, I was chiefly employed by the master in his garden, digging, planting, sowing, prun-ing and so forth. I also hired a piece of vacant garden ground from him, for which I paid him 6s., and planted it with potatoes. I intended to buy a pig in the autumn, feed it on these potatoes, and sell it in the spring. But that summer was so dry that nearly all kinds of vegetation, save wheat, were withered away. I did not get as many potatoes out of my piece of ground as were equal to the price I paid for it. So that my father's having also failed, I was but too glad to do for mine what I had intended a pig to do — eat them.[33]

Justified suspicion of the arguments advanced by late-nineteenth and early-twentieth-century proponents of working-class allotments must not be allowed to obscure the fact that both gardens and allotments could be made profitable. Fortunately oral and autobiographical evidence together with the social surveys carried out at the beginning of the present century do allow a reasonably balanced view to be arrived at. The surveys reveal that all over the country agricultural labourers were able to supplement their normal incomes by the sale of garden produce. In one year a North Riding labourer made nearly two pounds from sales of potatoes and gooseberries, while the sale of home-grown lettuces, onions and cabbages helped one Essex labourer to pay the six pounds rent for his cottage. Oral evidence confirms that in urban areas too allotments were seen by working people as a worthwhile investment: 'A penny packet of seeds or ha'penny whatever they may be. A packet of lettuce seeds cost a ha'penny and you'd get ha'penny each for the lettuce. It was quite a lot of money.'[34] For many the back garden or allotment was probably their introduction to the joys and sorrows of penny capitalism. A south Yorkshire boy remembers that he and his sisters

would sit round the fire, drawing up wonderful plans for raising more money. Amongst other schemes was one for selling the surplus produce from our garden; but, alas, there wasn't any surplus. When the spring came I took the spade and dug; then I found that even garden seed was not to be had without money. It was disappointing, for I had rare visions of what I could do in the market-garden business. However, I had made some pals at school, and they set me up with their dads' surplus garden seed. When summer came I had as good a show of weeds and plants as any one in the village. The village in those days was a popular resort for visitors, and my eldest sister — she was thirteen and always more practical than I ever was — got the idea of selling flowers. It was a come-down for a lad of twelve, but I have never since felt anything like the joy of having a fist full of money as when one Saturday afternoon we spilled eighteen pennies on the table, our first result of selling flowers.[35]

Livestock could also be made to pay. The sale of small birds and animals made a welcome contribution to the family budget: the *Smallholder* claimed to know in 1910 of a woman who had bought a black pom dog and bitch for six pounds, fed them on scraps, mated them and sold the puppies for £22. Rabbits and poultry were also relatively easy to look after. If the profit from hens was small, it was pointed out, 'their cost of maintenance is still less'.[36] Typical was the wife of an Essex agricultural labourer who in the years before the First World War reckoned to be able to make about a pound a year from her six hens. Less typical was the shepherd from near Maidstone who kept both hens and rabbits. The hens he kept for their eggs: 'We used to have a chart behind the coal cupboard door . . . that my father used to write out weekly, and we had an egg tin, one of those Gold Flake tins, to put the egg money in, because it was ploughed back into the meal, and the corn, and you would mark down on the day how many eggs you got.'[37] His chinchilla rabbits he bred for their pelts, using the money to pay the doctor's bills for his wife who suffered from a bad heart.[38]

It was the pig however which was considered the best of all animals for the garden and allotment. According to one authority, 'pig-keeping to the small farmer is the portion of his business which, considering the return, monopolises the least capital.'[39] The *Daily Express* was even more enthusiastic: 'the pig is "a savings bank which pays more than 25 per cent interest"'.[40] Pig-keeping was potentially profitable, it is true; but it was not without its risks. The agricultural market was rarely predictable: 'sometimes the meal would go up in price and the price of meat would go down, and by the time you'd get your pig fat the price of meal was up — you'd lose money on them then. Then another time it 'ud be the reverse. You had to take a chance.' Then there was the threat of swine fever and other diseases. Meery Kimber from Headington Quarry, outside Oxford, was particularly unlucky.

I have had the misfortune to lose my sow and eleven small pigs, I tried my best, so did the vetinary surgeons but it was no good, you see she has a slight cold and this caused her to farry a month before time. Its all gone and buried — as you know bacon is well up in price so is pigs these eleven and sow would have been worth £14 now I have lost all my whole summers work throwed away, its fairly knocked me up.

But the return from successful pig rearing could be substantial. At least two other pig keepers from Headington Quarry claimed that they used 'the money from them pigs' to buy houses.[41] More often, no doubt, the profit from the family pig was devoted to more mundane purchases.

'We get the clothes out of the pigs, or we should never have any.'
'What pigs?'
Then came the story of how, now four years ago, Walpole's brother had given him a 'reckling' — in other words, an abnormally small and fragile pig, which could only live if an abnormal amount of care and attention were given to it. This care the Walpoles gladly bestowed, and they succeeded with much difficulty in rearing the puny animal. They kept it for six months, then sold it, and bought two young pigs. By keeping two pigs for six months and selling them before the fattening time they make, to name the very outside figure, £4 yearly. Perhaps, to take average of the years, £3 10s. would be nearer the mark. But whatever they make is devoted to clothing for the whole family. No entry is made in the budget [compiled by the family] for the keep of these pigs, which live mainly on 'the children's scraps', cabbages, and bad potatoes.[42]

Gardening and allotment holding were among the most popular, not to say most successful, of the many manifestations of nineteenth and early-twentieth-century penny capitalist enterprise. Unfortunately it is no longer possible, if in-

deed it ever was, to estimate the exact number of working
people who used their gardens and allotments to produce for
the market. It is clear, however, that in both town and
country these small plots provided workmen with an important and generally profitable spare-time interest. Almost all
allotment holders sold some of their produce, while a substantial number worked chiefly for sale. Even the most market orientated small producer retained a most valuable fall-
back position whenever he was unable to sell his stock: he
and his family could always eat it. If few families ever made
their fortune from this low cost, part-time and unambitious
form of penny capitalism, then few at least ever suffered
irreparable loss.

The same cannot be said of smallholding. The transition
from tending a garden or allotment to running a fully fledged
smallholding could be traumatic. Whereas gardens and allotments were never intended to be more than mere adjuncts to
the domestic economy, the whole purpose of acquiring a
smallholding was to become self-supporting, to become independent of wage labour, to progress socially perhaps as well
as economically. Nonetheless fear of poverty remained as
potent a driving force as the desire for economic success. The
threat of destitution hung over all working people, and there
is little doubt that the fear of pauperism encouraged many to
hanker after land. Old age was especially perilous. Indeed by
the end of the century even late middle age was 'becoming a
serious drawback' in newly mechanised trades like shoemak-
ing. The result was that in Northamptonshire the tenants of
the Rushden Permanent Allotment and Small Holdings Society
were 'nearly all shoemakers. The larger plots are held by retired shoemakers or agricultural jobbing men, who go in for
dairying or market-gardening . . . a small holding has taken the
place of an old-age pension to those older men who are
getting displaced by younger labour.'[43] Similarly, it was said
of the Wiltshire village of Corsley at the beginning of this century that

> If a man loses an arm, becomes rheumatic, or in any way
> is so disabled as to have difficulty in finding an employer
> as an agricultural labourer, he cultivates his garden, perhaps
> manages to obtain a horse and cart, builds himself a rough

stable of corrugated iron and some pigstyes, and, working with his wife, manages to make a hard living, probably being reduced to dependence in his old age.[44]

Such strategies were only feasible of course in the countryside and in small towns, but it does seem that in all parts of the country middle-aged working people continued to view the ownership of land as one possible form of insurance against life's vicissitudes.

For others, ambition rather than fear was the motivating force. There is no doubt that the high value placed upon the ownership or occupation of land was often sentimental and unrealistic — or, to put it more kindly, that often it derived as much from social as from economic considerations. 'I was a guard on the railway three year back,' explained one smallholder early this century, 'and I used to pass up and down and look out on the land until I couldn't stand it no longer.'[45] Such land hunger did often contain a hard streak of realism. For many rural workers a smallholding represented their only possible means of escape, 'their one hope', however remote, 'of prosperity and independence'.[46] An early-twentieth-century investigator asked one smallholder how he had come to set up on his own.

Why, bless you, I worked twelve years as a labourer myself before I became a holder, and then it were quite by chance that I started on my own. It was the frost of '92 from which I reckons everything. Mr Martin had to give six of us the sack; I'd just taken three-quarters of an acre of ground too, to fill in my spare time. Well, the frost swep' all the blossom I had and shifted me from work too, so things looked pretty black all round. The only thing was to set to on my own bit o' land and look out for a new job. Well, in a few weeks I got a new job and 2s. a week more wages, which kept things going until I got a bit more land, for I see'd then the insecurity like of relying on an employer in a bad season. It was a black year all round. I only had two plums on my trees, and someone else ate they! Yet, it was the frost of '92 as just set me thinking and really put me on my feet.[47]

However desirable it might seem to become a smallholder,

it was inevitably a struggle to raise the necessary capital. Indeed the growing popularity of smallholdings made the dream increasingly difficult to realise. By the end of the nineteenth century it was no longer possible to reclaim land from the waste and it could cost as much as £6 an acre to rent a holding. So it took a well paid, middle-aged, thrifty and fortunate workman to accumulate the capital he needed from out of his weekly wages. The vast majority never even tried.[48] 'I don't want no small holding, sir', explained one agricultural labourer,

> why should I? — and besides, I ain't got the money to risk and put into the place. It's just as good as my own now, if I had a bit more pay. I does much as I likes and knows everything as goes on. It's not as if Mr Gordon didn't tell me things or seem contented like, but he always tells I what my lambs fetches and if a thing turns out good or bad. If I wants to keep a pig I've only got to ask him, and he knows as I looks to his pocket to save for 'im anyway. No, sir, I'm content to work for a good master like Mr Gordon.[49]

According to the agricultural press, there were three ways of raising the money for a smallholding: by saving, by buying a share in an existing holding, or by obtaining a loan on the security of a life insurance policy. Certainly it is not absolutely impossible to find examples of working men using what are generally regarded as middle-class financial institutions. There was, for example, the Kent shepherd and his wife who, by not spending '3d. where 2d. would do', eventually managed to raise a bank loan to add to their savings so that they were able to buy three cottages and thirty one acres of land for £350.[50] This, there can be no doubt, was quite exceptional. A more popular expedient was for enterprising workers to try to use their allotments as a means of acquiring smallholdings. Thus in the seed-growing district round Tiptree in Essex, the usual practice was said to be 'for the men to start with a ¼-acre allotment while still at regular work, and gradually to extend their holdings as they learn the art of growing and dressing the seed . . . If a man is then able to get 3 or 4 acres of land, he can give up regular work.'[51] It was also claimed to be not uncommon in the Vale of Evesham 'to find instances where steady, industrious labourers commence with an allotment; then take over a larger one; and in three or four years more we find these men fully developed market gardeners with their four, six, or ten acres of garden, horses and carts, and living in their own new, well-fitted, and well-furnished homes'.[52]

However it is only too easy to exaggerate the extent to which allotments provided that vital 'first rung in the rural social ladder'. It is important to remember the insistence of many contemporary commentators that it was almost impossible for a man to 'rise from the position of labourer and allotment holder to that of a small holder, without engaging in other business, but in the vast majority of cases a man attains the latter position by engaging first in some petty business. It is rather the village tradesman than the farm worker who is assisted by allotments to become a small holder or later a farmer.'[53] It is also important to remember that the 'first rung in the rural social ladder' was lower in some parts of the country than it was in others. In general the desire to own a smallholding was a more realistic ambition in arable districts than it could ever be in grasslands where farming required much greater capital investment. But even in a county like Norfolk, where the ladder was probably more easily climbed than in many other districts, the agricultural labourer still had to fight hard to get a foot onto the bottom rung. When the Norfolk Small Holdings Association established eighteen tenants on a colony at Whissonsett near Fakeham, six of those chosen were agricultural labourers; but these were easily outnumbered by a baker, a poulterer, a farmer's son, a pensioner, two smallholders and dealers, a shoemaker and carrier, an innkeeper and two carpenters. It was for the agricultural labourers that reformers agitated and politicans legislated. But if farm labourers were not the last in the queue for smallholdings, they were by no means the first. Everywhere the story was the same: the land market was always far less accessible to the low paid and the unskilled than it was to local artisans — sometimes of course already penny capitalists in another guise.[54]

It is not surprising that the distribution of smallholdings tended to be rather patchy. They clustered on the edges of towns and in 'districts specially suited for fruit or vegetables':

at Tiptree in Essex, near St Dominick in Cornwall, round
Upwey in Dorset and Rock in Worcestershire, in the Sandy-
Biggleswade area of Bedfordshire, on the Isle of Axholme,
round Evesham and on the Isle of Ely and Cambridgeshire
fruit belt. Fortunately for the historian, late-nineteenth and
early-twentieth-century interest in the land question makes it
no difficult matter to discover the total number of smallholdings that were under cultivation during this period. Between
1895 and 1909 the number of smallholdings (of one to five
acres) in England decreased slightly from just over 87,000 to
barely 80,000, but then rose again to about 88,000 by the
First World War. In 1908 England, Wales and Scotland together contained about 108,000 smallholdings.[55] Unfortunately, however, there is no way of assessing accurately the
proportion of these holdings which were run by penny capitalists. It would be hopelessly naive of course to assume that
smallholdings, like allotments, were normally run by working
people. The only way by which any sort of estimate can be
made is to assume that over the country as a whole working-
class involvement in smallholding was probably somewhat
lower than in districts like Evesham and Norfolk where
between a quarter and a third of smallholders seem to have
been working class. Such a calculation, it must be admitted,
is rather unreliable; but it does suggest that at the beginning
of the present century about twenty five to thirty five
thousand working-class families depended on smallholdings
for their livelihood. This is a figure which, while offering little
support for the view that smallholding was destroyed by
industrialisation, does contrast sharply with the total of well
over half a million families who were selling produce from
their gardens and allotments. It provides a striking indication
of the difficulty of expanding from part-time gardening to
nominally full-time smallholding.

Naturally the precise balance of production on any particular holding depended upon the prevailing climate and type
of soil, on transport facilities, consumer demand and upon
local custom. Certain generalisations can be made however.
Few smallholders grew corn because it was relatively cheap
to buy and because it depended 'on relatively simple mechanical processes, and makes no special demands on the in-

terest and industry of the labourer'. On the rare occasions when corn was grown, it was used almost entirely for domestic consumption, as fodder and straw or for making into bread. On the other hand, most smallholders grew fruit and vegetables and kept livestock: 'it appears that the relative number of cattle and pigs kept regularly decreases as the size of holding increases, but the sheep increase.'[56] Like pigs and poultry, cattle could be made a paying proposition and although it was generally reckoned that it needed three acres to keep a single cow, some penny capitalists made do with far less. The 1889 Select Committee on Smallholdings was told, for instance, of a farm labourer at Delamere in Cheshire who managed to keep four cows on his seven acres. Raising cattle for milk could be very profitable in or near large towns. London still had about 700 licensed cowhouses in the 1880s, before their monopoly was undermined by the introduction of 'railway milk'. Indeed it was said of turn of the century York that 'There is a marked absence of large dairy farms, the milk trade being in the hands of a large number of dairymen each owning a few cows. Some of these men possess only one or two cows, which are not infrequently kept under conditions far from satisfactory. A number of these small producers will sell their milk to one dealer, who undertakes its distribution.'[57]

Every smallholder organised his work differently. The Select Committee on Smallholdings learned in 1889 of a mason's labourer at Minster Lovell in Oxfordshire who lived on a two acre holding which he rented for nine pounds a year. Helped by his two sons, he grew roots, swedes, barley and mangolds for his own use, but bred pigs and grew potatoes for sale on the open market. Here is how another smallholder described his policy.

It's largely fruit and vegetables we depends on, but we have to go slow in planting fruit; it needs a bit of capital. Nearly all we smallholders have our pigs, and poultry, some on us, and all of us grows a half acre of wheat. Cone wheat mostly, 'cos we can't afford to feed the sparrows. There are six of us, the wife and me and four young 'uns, and that half acre keeps us in flour for bread and cakes and cooking for close on six months. It's what I calls really living off the land, money doesn't count so much then; with the wheat and a good side of bacon in the house, one looks forward to the winter all right. And all the summer one works much lighter, too; it's just as good as having summer all the year round like. We make a tidy bit off the vegetables and fruit, and saves a bit, too, and all the time we're knowing we're storing up the sun in the wheat for winter time.[58]

The distribution of his produce was much more of a worry for the smallholder than it was for the gardener or allotment holder. 'When starting business, the small holder may use either the prevailing methods of marketing his particular kind of produce, or find a market for himself. The latter is often a difficult and sometimes a costly process, requiring both patience and capital.'[59] Accordingly the smallholder often began by turning, almost instinctively it seems, to the simple procedures which had sufficed when he had been working a garden or allotment. Like the allotment holder he would sell small quantities from the back door or hawk his produce round the streets. A Wolverhampton gardener acquired a cottage and two acres of land in June 1910 and immediately took on a part-time job delivering eggs and poultry for a friend. This gave him the opportunity to sell his own produce and by the end of the year he had managed to build up a round of about thirty customers for his eggs, potatoes, poultry and vegetables. It was common too for smallholders to take their goods to market. In north Devon, for instance, it was 'the regular practice for the wives and daughters of the small farmers . . . to take poultry, eggs, butter and clotted cream, as well as garden produce, honey etc., into the market once a week and there sell it direct to the customers'.[60]

These time-consuming, traditional methods of marketing were not always able to cope adequately with the volume of produce emanating from even a modest smallholding. Indeed the limitations of both the hawker's round and the local market became more serious as smallholders began to face growing competition from Continental food producers after about 1875. Thus by the end of the century more and more smallholders, particularly the smaller ones, were trying to divest themselves of their direct responsibility for distribution. 'They sell either to large farmers, or to artisans, or small shop-keepers, inn-keepers, etc.' Whatever means they adopted, all the evidence suggests that most smallholders managed to cope reasonably well with the disposal of their produce.[61]

It has been seen already that it is notoriously difficult to determine the profitability of any penny capitalist enterprise. For one thing, it is almost impossible to calculate the extent of hired help and of unpaid family labour. It is clear, however, that in smallholding this varied according to the family life cycle: a man with young children or a pregnant wife would probably have to work alone, whereas twenty years later he might be helped both by his wife and by one or more of his grown up children. A second difficulty derives from the fact that, despite their dreams of independence, many smallholders had to resort to other ways of supplementing their income, at least during certain periods of the year. Thus the success of the Tiptree holdings was attributed to the ease with which they could be used as adjuncts to employment in the local jam and fruit growing industry. Similarly it was found that between Bromsgrove and Kidderminster 'many who are said to be making an entire living on the land, earn their extra money in actual connection with small holdings — viz., by buying other supplies . . . and bringing back in their empty carts loads of manure to sell after taking the produce into Birmingham.'[62]

Nonetheless it is clear that many difficulties stood between the smallholder and a successful enterprise. Economies of scale were impossible, rents were often high and the land sometimes remote and unsuitable. Here is an early-twentieth-century description of one such unpromising site.

Only recently I crossed from one fertile river-bed over the high hills to another rich alluvial plain. It was on the bleak top of these hills where I found 'the land for the people', as glaring notice boards announced it. Some acres of young standard fruit trees had been set out in preparation for the unwary small man, and to complete their destruction, the ground had been laid down to their very trunks with a heavy crop of rye grass! The farmers in the valleys smiled and shrugged their shoulders; none of them, with ample capital and sound practical knowledge as landowners or tenants, would make venture of such an industry on these exposed and isolated hilltops. Yet it is the land set apart for the people, who have saved a small sum after years of toil, and are feeling their way back to the earth. As usual, they will get a rough awakening and their last hope will be shattered.[63]

Even a central, accessible position was not an unmixed blessing. Urban holdings posed their own particular difficulties. There was the ever present threat of pilfering, poaching, pollution, vandalism and stray dogs while the possibility of land speculation was unlikely to encourage the landlord to undertake any long-term investment. In Sheffield, for example, a combination of poor land and industrial dirt and smoke ensured that yields always remained low. A further difficulty for all smallholders was the unpredictability of any form of agricultural enterprise. The best laid plans were likely to be set at naught by changes in the weather and variations in demand. The first eighteen months were the worst. 'When the labourer becomes a small holder he changes the condition of dependence on employment and his employer for dependence on the weather, the market, and sometimes on the merchant or the auctioneer.'[64]

In these circumstances failures were only too common. A Warwickshire woman remembered her 'plan to start William towards independence. She had a little money and he could have it to buy a cow and a pig. He did so, but calamity befell the animals.'[65] A Wiltshire railway worker recalled that

> During the many years I have spent in the works I have known of but one case in which a man left the shed to go back to the land as a small working farmer. He had always been careful and thrifty, and seemed to be well fitted for the agricultural life, but he could not succeed in it. After five or six years of hard labour, trying in vain to prosper, he returned to the shed, a disappointed and ruined man: he had spent his savings and lost the whole of his small capital. He is still working in the shed, and he has no intention of repeating the experiment.[66]

Yet profits were made. Near large towns even unsuitable sites could be made to pay and it has been argued recently that 'Very small occupiers who produced partly for subsistence, or who sold a specialized or perishable produce like milk, hops or vegetables on a sheltered local market, might be in a favoured position'.[67] The contemporary literature resounds to stories of successful smallholdings.

> Mr B— is the son of a boot and shoemaker, and started life in the same trade, under his father, as soon as he could toddle about. He left the trade at the early age of eleven, taking to farm labouring and blacksmithing, as a journeyman workman, until about his twenty-fifth year, when he took to nail-making and gardening jointly, making his nails in an ordinary labourer's cottage on his own account. By much perseverance, thrift, and care, he was able gradually to extend his allotment ground, and whilst doing this he gradually decreased his labour as a nailer, which was becoming, as now, more and more an extinct trade, and unprofitable withal. As an allotment holder, he started with a quarter acre of ground, which he increased to half an acre, and then to one acre. Bit by bit he increased the size of his holding, until at the present time he occupies no less than 15 acres. Mr B— is a typical son of the soil, both as regards appearance and robustness of health: he has 'money in the bank', and he intends to add, as soon as he can procure them, another 10 to 20 acres to his 15.[68]

It is certainly the case that during the second half of the nineteenth century changing patterns of consumption worked to the advantage of the smallholder. More and more of rising working-class incomes came to be spent on semi-luxuries such as meat, vegetables, flowers, fruit and dairy produce, most of which could be grown profitably on small acreages.[69] But it is important not to exaggerate the profitability of smallholding. Many smallholders, like those near Plymouth, probably had to be content 'to live themselves on that which is not so easily converted into money'. Most made only modest profits. The margin of safety was precariously narrow, the difference between comfort and poverty one piece of bad luck. 'When the agricultural labourer becomes a small farmer, he often exchanges moderate hours and regular wages for incessant toil and a meagre competency.'[70]

Working-class enterprise in the primary sector of the economy shared many of the characteristics common to all types of penny capitalism. It survived largely unrecognised, particularly on a part-time basis, in those parts of industry which received little capital investment or underwent relatively little technological change. Thus both fishing and smallholding continued to provide nominally full-time employment to a small number of penny capitalists, holding out to them inspiring (if often quite illusory) dreams of economic and even of social success. Much more important, both fishing and gardening continued to offer wage-earners the opportunity to make some extra money in their spare time. Compared to full (or nearly full) time penny capitalism, this part-time enterprise was far more common, considerably less ambitious, and much more successful. Yet the low initial capital cost was not an unmixed blessing: while it facilitated working-class entry into business, especially on a part-time basis, it made it all the more difficult to withstand any sort of economic adversity. This was a paradox which was to recur in whichever sector of the economy penny capitalism entered.

4

Manufacturing

The manufacturing sector of the economy, like the primary, provided working people with a number of outlets for their entrepreneurial ambitions; but textiles and the heavy industries were not among these. True, it was often said of the early nineteenth century cotton industry that 'any young man who was industrious and careful might . . . from his earnings as a weaver lay by sufficient to set him up as a manufacturer' and that it was common to attribute depressions in the industry to the ease with which workmen, with little capital, were able to enter the ranks of the employers.[1] Yet in textiles, as in every other field of penny capitalist endeavour, the historian must not allow himself to be seduced by well known, though quite untypical, stories of entrepreneurial success. For every James Gledhill or David Whitehead who climbed from poverty to prosperity, there were dozens who floundered and thousands, if not tens of thousands, more who never 'had the courage to embark in the attempt'.[2] Whatever opportunities may have existed in the early years of the Industrial Revolution, there is no doubt that in textiles, as in mining, these declined sharply as time wore on. The intensification of competition together with the prohibitive cost of even the cheapest machinery meant that by as early as 1833 it was said to be impossible 'for industrious men of good character and prudence, without capital' to borrow sufficient money to set up in cotton spinning.[3] Thwarted in their entrepreneurial ambitions, Lancashire cotton workers comforted themselves with the local proverb about their more dynamic neighbours who went 'from clogs to clogs in only three generations'.[4]

Fortunately for the ambitious workman, other branches of manufacturing industry were better able to satisfy penny capitalist aspirations. In craft trades such as clothing, shoe-making, furniture assembly, net-making and food preparation and even in artisan trades like engineering and metal-working, rising demand was met not by that mechanisation and con-centration of production so characteristic of the staple industries, but by the proliferation of any number of small, labour-intensive units which remained largely unchanged by industrialisation.[5]

Even working people without any formal training and with next to no capital could begin some form of craft production on a part-time basis. Often the necessary raw materials could be obtained for absolutely nothing. Early-nineteenth-century Swaledale lead miners used to gather fallen wool which they carded, spun and knitted into stockings, while throughout the period gypsies were able to make clothes pegs from the wood which they collected. A Dover boy remembers that when he and his labourer father used to make nets at the end of the last century, it was possible to buy a large ball of string for a halfpenny.

> But I used to be all round the dustbins, there was any amount of string laying about then. I used to bring it home, all home, take it all to pieces. Sit there at night time, take it all to pieces, especially if it was cold and rainy. Make it up into balls. He used to sit there and knit them. Cabbage net was like that, two inch or inch and a half mesh, and sprout meshes would be a bit smaller. And they used to cook in them, in their big pots, in the houses. And potatoes. Used to get about 2*d*. or 3*d*. each for them.[6]

Even when capital equipment and raw materials did have to be bought, they were probably not very expensive. At the beginning of this century, for example, one Hull man used his spare time to make pieces of wire into baskets for hanging plants and to pickle onions and red cabbage for resale to local shopkeepers. Meanwhile, recalls a girl from Barrow-in-Furness,

> We had another woman who used to sell pop. She used to make pop and she used to sell ha'penny bottles of pop and penny bottles of pop. She used to brew it and put the yeast on the top and it used to come up. She used to send it to the works, Steel Works, and the men used to come

and buy half a dozen bottles of pop and it used to fly up
like champagne.[7]

In other parts of the country some working people were
able to raise the larger sums of money needed to manufacture
more potent drinks. In the early-nineteenth-century Highlands
of Scotland it was said to cost less than four pounds to purchase all the equipment necessary for the pot-still distillation
of whisky, while the grain could usually be bought on credit
from local farmers. Indeed illegal activities such as this were
well suited to part-time, penny capitalist production because
it was so much easier to avoid detection when they were
carried out in the privacy of the family.[8]

Many women, of course, were able to turn their day-to-
day domestic skills to good account. Despite the growing
importance of cheap, mass-produced clothing during the
second half of the century, there remained a substantial — if
easily overlooked — local market for women willing to take
in sewing and dressmaking, especially for alteration and
repair. Indeed such enterprise was encouraged by the increasing availability and decreasing cost of the domestic sewing
machine, which was perfected in its modern form in 1846.
By the end of the century it was not generally too difficult
for the working-class woman to obtain a machine, on hire
purchase perhaps or by joining forces with her mother or
daughter. The best laid plans could go astray however: a
Manchester hire purchase salesman said to one woman, ' "Will
you have a sewing machine?" she said "Oh I can't pay for a
sewing machine", he said, "Well I'll tell you what, will you
come and do my wife's washing, and I'll put one and six a
week on a card for you", so she went and did the week's
washing for them every Monday,' but the salesman died
before the machine was paid for.[9]

Sometimes the initial impetus for taking in work came
from a particular family crisis: the daughter of a Wigan miner
remembers that in about 1910 'they were out on strike and
my mother always had a sewing machine, and many a time
we had nothing for breakfast. Before we went to school my
mother would run a pinnie up for a little girl for sixpence.'[10]
More often the impetus derived simply from the unending
shortage of money, from the desire to find any part-time job

which promised to fit reasonably easily into the domestic routine. Often it caused friction however. The wife of a labourer at the Vickers company in Barrow-in-Furness used to take in sewing:

> Sometimes she never got paid and she never charged very much when she did get paid but often she never got paid. M'dad used to worry with her having all the babies and he'd see her sewing and sewing. One time he picked it up and put it on the fire because it got him down so much.[11]

Despite such domestic difficulties and in spite of the growth of the mass-production clothing industry, many woman did continue with part-time home dressmaking and repair. What little evidence there is suggests that the numbers taking in sewing around the turn of the century varied between about seven and twelve per cent of all married working-class women.[12]

Men with specialised artisan skills were still more favourably placed to undertake production in their spare time. Skilled workers like watchmakers, joiners, tailors and cobblers commonly took orders and did repairs for their friends and neighbours. Sometimes they even managed to do the work in their employers' time. When a fire broke out at the tailoring firm of Redpath and Manning in Bond Street, London in the winter of 1866, it was found that 'Trade being very dull at present in that establishment, a number of the workmen had garments in the shop which they were making either for themselves or their friends'.[13] The boot and shoe industry too remained a fruitful field for part-time, and even full-time, enterprise. The introduction of the sewing machine in mid-century allowed some workmen to break free from the out-work system and set up as independent manufacturers. But the emergence of modern factory production during the final quarter of the century finally forced penny capitalists to abandon manufacturing in favour of repair. A South Wales miner recalls,

> In those days boot repairers were numerous, for it was a craft very much in demand. Boots and shoes were made to last then and were in comparison much more expensive than their modern mass-produced counterpart, being repaired again and again in their long life. Boots at that

time were handed down from one member of the family to another. Children were like well-shod horses galloping around the place, and their footwear had to be strong to stand up to the rough, unsurfaced roads of those days.[14]

So just before the First World War a jobbing gardener, who had once lodged with a bootmaker, used to go round from door to door at Farsely on the outskirts of Leeds to collect boots for repair, while in a Swindon railway factory there worked a man who 'was at one time a cobbler, and used to get up his living by the patching up and renovation of old soles. Long after he entered the shed he kept up the employment in his spare time.'[15]

It was only slightly more expensive for skilled workers to embark upon a fully fledged penny capitalist career. Indeed one choice facing any artisan was whether to work for an employer or to try to go it alone. Some, no doubt, opted for penny capitalism as their chief means of support because they wanted an improved standard of living, a greater degree of independence, or the satisfaction of being responsible for the entire process of production. Most, however, were less ambitious: they chose penny capitalism simply because they had little alternative. In fact, it is striking how throughout the nineteenth century and beyond every rise in unemployment drove skilled men into self-employment. During the first half of the century even metal and engineering workers managed to begin independent, or quasi-independent, production. Thus during the slump which followed the Napoleonic Wars and again during the depression of the 1840s and 1850s unemployed artisans with little if any capital managed to set up their own small workshops in engineering centres such as Birmingham, Wolverhampton and Sheffield.[16]

Although opportunities in engineering and metal-working declined during the second half of the century, they remained common in traditional, labour-intensive branches of manufacturing such as coffin making, bag sewing, box making, coining and cabinetmaking.[17] Clothing was another such industry. The ease with which it remained possible to set up as a small master (or mistress) helps to explain the continuing appeal of this trade to immigrants and other disadvantaged groups. All that was needed was a room, some materials, and a sewing machine which could be either hired or bought on hire purchase. Early this century an elderly London woman explained how she had worked for a West End firm of dress-makers for fifteen years before it went bankrupt. Unable to find work elsewhere because of her age, she began to make babies' frocks from material bought cheaply in the local market and managed to sell them to neighbours who fortunately did not seem to 'mind how many joins there are'.[18] So neither financial constraints nor technical demands acted as major disincentives to entry at some level into this hidden world of penny capitalist manufacturing.

Ironically, it was precisely this low threshold of entry which presented penny capitalist manufacturers with their most severe difficulties. Immigrants and unemployed workers flooded in. As late as 1911 six per cent of male French polishers, ten per cent of tailors and upholsterers, thirteen per cent of wheelwrights, and a third of watch and clock repairers described themselves in the census as workers on their own account. It is not easy to assess the impact which the survival of this form of nominally full-time manufacturing had upon particular communities. Charles Booth's work does allow the historian to analyse the scattered evidence of small-scale manufacturing in one part of the capital. In his survey of east London and Hackney in the late 1880s, Booth discovered that a considerable number of families worked on their own account. Fathers worked as bootmakers, tailors, clock and watch repairers, locksmiths and picture-frame makers, while whole families worked together at firewood cutting or at slipper and toy making. In all, calculated Booth, some 2.2 per cent of the population in this part of the capital was dependent upon home industries and small workshops.[19]

Such ease of entry produced serious overcompetition. This in turn encouraged inexperienced workers to undervalue their products and made life difficult for even the most accomplished. Indeed overcompetition was far more of a problem for the small manufacturer than it was for, say, the small-holder. As Mayhew pointed out long ago, when discussing the 'garret masters' in the London cabinet trade:

They are in manufacture what 'the peasant proprietors' are in agriculture — their own employers and their own workmen. There is, however, this one marked distinction between the two classes — the garret master cannot, like the peasant proprietor, *eat* what he produces; the consequence is, that he is obliged to convert each article into food immediately he manufactures it — no matter what the state of the market may be. The capital of the garret master being generally sufficient to find him in materials for the manufacture of only one article at a time, and his savings being but barely enough for his subsistence while he is engaged in putting those materials together, he is compelled, the moment the work is completed, to part with it for whatever he can get. He cannot afford to keep it even a day, for to do so is generally to remain a day unfed. Hence, if the market be at all slack, he has to force a sale by offering his goods at the lowest possible price . . . Moreover, it is well known how strong is the stimulus among peasant proprietors, or, indeed, any class working for themselves, to extra production. So it is, indeed, with the garret masters; their industry is almost incessant, and hence a greater quantity of work is turned out by them, and continually forced into the market, than there would otherwise be. What though there be a brisk and a slack season in the cabinet-maker's trade as in the majority of others? — slack or brisk, the garret masters must produce the same excessive quantity of goods. In the hope of extricating himself from his over-whelming poverty, he toils on, producing more and more — and yet the more he produces the more hopeless does his position become; for the greater the stock that he thrusts into the market, the lower does the price of his labour fall, until at last, he and his whole family work for less than half what he himself could earn a few years back by his own unaided labour.[20]

Not surprisingly, overcompetition, shortage of capital and inexperience made it difficult for penny capitalist manufacturers to cope with even the normal vagaries of trade. Often, of course, workers went into business just when — and precisely because — trade was bad. As the wife of an east London tailor explained at the beginning of this century, she only took in home dressmaking when her husband's trade was slack, 'but says that in slack times [people] don't have clothes made'.[21] Even the profits made by apparently full-time penny capitalists rarely resulted in economic security, let alone in any upward social mobility. In fact, it was often said of the early-nineteenth-century metal and engineering trades that many journeymen who had become small masters would willingly have returned to their former jobs if they could have been sure of full employment at good wages. Those in the handicraft trades also faced increasingly severe competition from the large multiple stores.

> Bob Eastham's father had a tailoring business. They were, of course, feeling the loss of business. This however was put down to the Jews and Burton the tailor. Bob's greatest pleasure was to get us to stand looking into a Burton shop window, he had found out that an assistant when not otherwise engaged stood on a ladder to look over the window back. If he saw anyone looking interested he would come outside to try to get you into the shop. Bob would waste his time by making all types of enquiries, then insult him.[22]

The effect of such precarious and vulnerable penny capitalism upon trade-union activity in the manufacturing sector is difficult to assess. On the one hand, some mid-Victorian union leaders welcomed penny capitalism as a possible avenue of individual advance for their members. In 1866, for example, a representative of the South Western Branch of the London Operative Tailors' Protective Association 'advised the men to commence business on their own account, as many of them could cut better than their employer'.[23] On the other hand, most union leaders came to see penny capitalism as a threat to the very foundations of trade-union organisation. It depleted their membership: at least three of the twenty eight London moulders excluded from their union for the non-payment of contributions during the first half of 1852 were said to have 'turned master', while twenty years later it was reported that 'Brother Watkins, vice-chairman of Greenwich boilermakers, was now a small employer'.[24] Penny capitalism also weakened union industrial policies: right to the end of the century small masters in the Sheffield cutlery trades were being accused of sweating their workmen and of undercutting both wages and prices. Increasingly, it seems, trade-union leaders came to abhor the effect which the small master and the penny capitalist had upon the working class as a whole. 'What is really important for working men,' it was pointed out in 1880, 'is, not that a few should rise out of their class — this sometimes rather injures the class by depriving it of more energetic members. The truly vital interest is that the whole class should rise in material comfort and security, and still more in moral and intellectual attainments.'[25]

'Material comfort and security' were hardly ever found by worker capitalists in textiles or any of the other heavy manufacturing industries. Indeed such openings as did exist shrank significantly with the growing capitalisation and concentration of production which became such striking features of this part of the economy. Nor were 'material comfort and security' won very often by penny capitalists in the handicraft sector. In fact the entry of workers into independent production was as likely to represent downward mobility as it was a move up the economic or social scale. This is not to deny of course that the labour-intensive handicraft sector was stimulated by the industrialisation process or that it continued to offer working men and women a whole range of penny capitalist opportunities. Indeed their acceptance of these opportunities is crucial to any understanding of either the reality of working-class life or of the nature of manufacturing industry in the nineteenth and early twentieth centuries.[26]

5

Building

The building industry was as well suited as the handicraft trades to penny capitalist ambition. Building work had always to be done *in situ* and there were few opportunities for employers to develop techniques of mass production. Moreover the industry remained essentially labour intensive so that the capital cost of starting even a full-time business was never very high. (It is still said of the building industry today that a craftsman can set up on his own armed with little more than a plank and a barrow.) Nineteenth-century craftsmen such as joiners, bricklayers and stone-masons managed to raise the capital they needed in a number of ways: they could barter their own work in exchange for labour and materials; they could seek loans from family, friends and local landowners and builders' merchants; or they could fall back on their own savings, if they had any. It was noticed in the 1870s, for instance, that a number of joiners and masons in Ashton-under-Lyne were saving with building societies in the hope of being able to start business on their own account. In the 1890s, recalled Rowland Kenney, his friend

> Fred learned of a possible job at Standish, a few miles the other side of Wigan. A local small contractor had been offered the job of building a couple of cottages for two miners who had come by some money and decided to build homes which would have bathrooms and be a considerable cut above the small places in which most of the local miners lived. The 'contractor' was a joiner who had the sense to see that there was going to be some building development in the neighbourhood, and that he would do better contracting than following his trade as a journeyman joiner; but he had no knowledge of bricklaying and

he wanted some assistance. It suited him better to sub-let
the bricklaying part of the job, and here was where I could
be useful. I was 'quick at figures', and Fred was not; so
the suggestion was that he should contract to do the brickwork at so much a square yard. I should be the labourer
and also do the measuring-up and generally act as clerk of
the works. As occasion served I was gradually to take over
a trowel. We had visions of becoming masters instead of
men, and tramping and roughing it seemed likely to be
things of the past for me.[1]

Thus it was often as easy for the craftsman to find his
own work as it was to look for an employer. Small jobs and
repairs were not difficult for a handy man. 'Formal training
was not necessary in order to put up or repair a stretch of
garden wall, to lay a cesspit, mend a roof, or build a pig-
sty.'[2] Nor was the small builder embarking on more ambitious
projects as his major source of income left without helpful
advice. By mid-century the technical press was supplying
complete kits of house-building designs together with bills
of quantities and other relevant information. With brickwork
comprising some forty per cent of the average finished house
and carpentry and joinery another thirty per cent, it was
relatively easy for either bricklayers or carpenters to organise
construction. The result was that the house building and
repair industry always contained a large number of small, and
often transitory, undertakings. Towns with a strong building
society movement and those, like Nottingham and London,
where leasehold tenure was common seem to have been
particularly conducive to these marginal jobbing firms with
little capital. In late-nineteenth-century London, for example,
a third of all house builders built only one or two houses a
year. Nor was the situation very different over the country as
a whole. According to the 1851 census of England and Wales
about a sixth of all firms of carpenters and joiners employed
just one man, while in 1891 about half the 47,000 employers
of carpenters, joiners, bricklayers, masons and plasterers were
listed as self-employed. In both London and the provinces
there were a very great number of 'small jobbing builders
who broke off now and then from their repairs and alterations
to put up a house or two'.[3]

As in manufacturing, the low capital cost of entry itself posed serious difficulties. For just as every rise in unemployment drove craftsmen to set up as small masters, so at the same time it encouraged downward bidding for building contracts. Unrealistic bidding soon shattered Rowland Kenney's dreams of independence: 'Whether we had taken on the job too cheaply I do not know — the amount Fred had asked per square yard struck me at the time as remarkably small, but he had been very reassuring when I questioned him about it and, after all, he said he "knew if anybody did" — but the job never paid even full wages.'[4] In the main, however, the small builder's problems arose not from such miscalculations of costs and profitability, but from shortages of cash.

A breakdown may come in various ways. Sometimes the builder goes bankrupt before the work is finished. He may fail to complete a particular stage of the building in the specified time, and so lose the instalment of the advance and be unable to pay his men. He must then either borrow money at interest or give up the job. If the financier is a man whose object is to foreclose, there are various ways in which he can turn the system to his advantage. Supposing that it is the condition of an advance that the house shall be roof-high by the end of the week, such a man will arrange to go round late on Friday, and if the house is not roof-high he will refuse the instalment. The builder who counted on being allowed to complete the stage on Saturday morning cannot pay his men, and the unfinished house falls to the financier, who gets nearly a whole week's work for nothing. Or the collapse may be caused by the pressure of the merchants to whom the builder is in debt for materials. They are liable to bear the losses of the transaction, for the financier has a prior claim to subsequent mortgagees, builders' merchants, &c.[5]

Small builders resilient enough to withstand such financial pitfalls had still other problems to contend with. Their independence, like that of many penny capitalist manufacturers, was often more apparent than real. Although small jobbers always dominated the industry numerically, they tended to become increasingly subordinated to the new, large, general contractors, for whom they provided a whole range of subcontracting services. Then there were the vagaries of the British climate. For certain periods of the year any form of outdoor work was difficult if not impossible. But employment prospects did not necessarily follow the seasons in any predictable fashion. Surprisingly perhaps, Christmas could usually be relied upon to produce some indoor work. Thus in the late autumn of 1879 paper-hangers and decorators in Wolverhampton were reported to be 'looking forward cheerfully to the latter end of November and to December as likely to bring them the customary amount of work which, at that season, is usually forthcoming by the determination of shopkeepers and householders to brighten up their premises and residences for Christmastide'.[6] All over the country the consequences of such fluctuations were similar: so even today one Lancaster woman's memories of the decade before the First World War stress the seasonal unemployment suffered by her father and uncle who worked together as self-employed painters and decorators.[7]

In spite of such uncertainties, for which building has always been notorious, the industry did continue to provide openings for the ambitious and desperate alike either to do a few jobs in their spare time or to try to make a small, jobbing business into their major source of income. This, it has been claimed, was of the very greatest importance. 'The persistence of a large number of small firms, and the extent of social mobility between employers and employed, masked the social relations of capitalist production, with the employers as property owners and the workers as the propertyless.'[8] Whatever the truth of the matter, there is no doubt that the building industry, like the handicraft trades, did provide escape for some and — much more important — assistance for many.

Despite the growth of the secondary sector of the economy (which by 1851 employed over forty per cent of the working population and contributed more than forty per cent of the national income), it never offered working people the same opportunities as the primary sector for entry into part-time penny capitalism. This was not only because building and manufacturing lacked the basic appeal of farming or fishing, but also because they made marginally higher demands of both capital and of skill. On the other hand, the secondary sector did offer skilled workmen and women more chance to make penny capitalism their chief means of support. It is important, of course, not to exaggerate the extent of these opportunities: indeed it is striking that not one of the penny capitalists identified from Elizabeth Roberts' oral investigations in Lancashire was ever active in either manufacturing or in building. Nonetheless, the secondary sector appeared much more open than the primary and there were always many more full-time (or nearly full-time) penny capitalist builders, tailors, cabinetmakers and boot and shoemakers than there were fishermen and smallholders.

6

Transport

Of all the many consequences of industrialisation, one of the most significant was undoubtedly the growing separation of the consumer both from the primary producer of raw materials and from the secondary manufacturer of finished goods. This widening gap came to be filled by an expanding and increasingly specialised tertiary (or service) sector, the emergence of which constitutes a striking, though still strangely neglected, feature of modern economic and social development.[1] It was in this tertiary sector of the economy, particularly in the provision of personal and retail services, that penny capitalists were at their most active.

It is well known that population growth, industrialisation and urbanisation all place increasingly severe demands upon a nation's transportation system. Indeed the expansion of the transport network has long been recognised as one of the central themes of nineteenth and early-twentieth-century British economic and social history. But transport historians, like those concerned with the primary and secondary sectors, have always tended to direct their attention towards the larger, more heavily capitalised undertakings for which most evidence survives.

Naturally working people could never hope to build railways or run ocean-going ships. More surprisingly, perhaps, few workmen ever managed to play much part in the movement of freight and passengers around the coast or along the growing network of canals. There were, of course, some opportunities on the coast. But as was seen in an earlier chapter, it was not always very easy to secure the use of a rowing boat or sailing vessel. Moreover the first was too small to carry cargo, while for most of the nineteenth century the other could probably be put to more profitable use on the inshore fishing grounds. It was only with the development of seaside resorts towards the end of the century that the small boat owner came into his own. Working men, like other local owners, helped to satisfy the visitors' craving for nautical amusement. By the 1880s Scarborough Council had licensed a hundred small pleasure boats and Morecambe a hundred more. By the beginning of the present century many fishermen at Deal, the headquarters of the British Sea Anglers' Society, were finding it more profitable to cater for anglers than it was to go out fishing.[2]

Nor did working people play a much more prominent role on inland waterways. As on the coast, the initial difficulty was to obtain the use of a boat. By the beginning of this century a twenty five to thirty ton Birmingham narrow boat was said to cost £65 and to last only between fifteen and twenty years. Some canal boatmen eliminated the cost — if not the risk — by using their employers' boats for their own part-time ventures; others hired boats or obtained them through membership of boat building societies. Unfortunately there is no way of discovering precisely how many working boatmen did manage to acquire a boat of their own. What is known, however, is that from mid-century onwards the number of bargemen, watermen and lightermen in England and Wales hovered around the 30,000 mark and that of these no more than five or six per cent (2,000 at the very most) ever worked on their own account. There is no way of knowing what proportion of these 2,000 owner-boatmen (or 'number ones') were working class. Even if it is assumed — most improbably — that half the 'number ones' had emerged from the ranks of working boatmen, this still means that there were never more than a thousand penny capitalists plying for hire along the canals of England and Wales.[3]

This national figure is slightly misleading, however, for in certain parts of the country penny capitalist boatmen faced little competition from either the companies owning the canals or from large carrying companies like Pickfords. On the Thames, in the East Midlands, and on the Mersey and Weaver in north-west England the 'number ones' (and presumably therefore working-class 'number ones') were able to secure a considerably greater share of trade than the national figures would suggest. Between 1879 and 1884 'number ones' accounted for a quarter of the canal boats registered at Hinckley (on the Ashby-de-la-Zouch canal), a third of those at Daventry, and as many as forty per cent of those registered at Tring (both of which were on the Grand Junction). Although the West Midlands trade was dominated generally by large carriers, the Birmingham area with its small-scale businesses apparently remained well suited to penny capitalist carrying. Thus it was said in 1886 that 'A great many of the men who navigate the Worcester Canal bring cargoes of hay and straw which are entirely their own venture. They buy it themselves — bring it to Birmingham and sell it; and take back with them a cargo of coal from the Black Country in return.'[4]

As in the other sectors of the economy, the small operator faced particular difficulties. His lack of capital made it difficult to repair minor accidents to the boat, cope with the death of his horse, surmount trade depressions, or survive bad weather like the severe frost which closed the canals in the early months of 1895. Harry Hanson has put the matter succinctly.

> Owner-boatmen and small operators lived in a perpetually precarious situation. They were usually restricted to the least profitable of all goods; they were subject to discrimination by canal companies; they often had to rely upon hirings from the larger carriers to exist and they were the first to be cast off in times of slump; they were restricted to the crumbs which fell from the tables of canal giants, even though, in some areas, these crumbs might be substantial ones; and, at the same time, anything from a horse's broken leg to a protracted frost could bring speedy ruin.[5]

It was on the land, rather than on the water, that working men (though hardly any women) contributed towards providing the transport facilities on which the country so much depended. Economic expansion stimulated demand for the movement of goods and people, a demand which could be met at the very simplest level by sedan-chairs or even by the use of home-made carts and barrows. The simple soap-box cart has fascinated generations of boys and it has never been more than a short step from using it as a plaything to regarding it as a means of making money. A Dover man remembers that

> When I was a boy, when I was at school, my ambition first was to get a pair of pram wheels and when I got a pair of pram wheels I wanted a Tate sugar box, those wooden Tate sugar boxes. I got one of them, got the bolts and made a barrow. I used to pick up four bags from the old girls in the street, on a Friday night, and their tanners, and I used to walk from there right up . . . to the gas house there, four bags of coke . . . And you got a farthing each for a bag. Go up there and get them. So that made you a penny. Then I used to go to the Cause is Altered pub with my little barrow, and I used to have to take all the bottles of stout and the beer to the old girls in the Gorley alms houses, their weekly orders. I would take them all round. Well, sometimes I got a farthing for one, but I generally used to come back with a bag of cakes, one would give you a fleed cake and another would give you a currant cake and another one another bit of cake, instead of giving you a halfpenny, because they hadn't got it, you know.[6]

Occasionally adults, too, were able to set such simple vehicles to profitable use. It was reported in 1889 that a man wearing a porter's badge was charging a shilling and more for wheelbarrow rides on Hampstead Heath and two years later it was revealed that over half the wheelchair proprietors and attendants in the country were self-employed.[7]

Of course any workman with real aspirations to making a full-time living by the movement of people or goods had somehow to acquire the use of a horse and the appropriate vehicle. The cost, though, was a great deterrent. By the end of the nineteenth century the price of either a new cab or of a horse and cart was between fifty and sixty pounds, an enormous sum for any working man to find. Not surprisingly therefore the normal practice in the late-Victorian and Edwardian cab trade was for drivers not to become truly independent operators, but to hire a cab daily from proprietors who controlled the trade. In London in the 1870s 'The charge for one Hansom and two horses per day varies from 10*s*. to 12*s*. in the dull season; but there are no less than eight "rises" in the course of the year . . . From the meeting of Parliament up to the Derby-day the price of cabs steadily increases; and, on the race-day itself, proprietors generally demand £1 15*s*. to £2 before they allow one of their cabs to go to Epsom.'[8] The system, for all its faults, did at least allow ambitious drivers to learn the trade while trying to save the money to purchase a cab of their own. There was no such means of entry into the carrying trade. Very occasionally however, cash grants were made to victims of industrial accidents to enable them to set up in a small way of business. Thus in 1890 the Bestwood Iron and Coal Company of Nottingham subscribed twenty pounds towards the fund which had been formed to buy a horse and cart for one of its injured miners. But for the most part the carrying trade was accessible only to those, like smallholders, who already owned their own horse and cart. In fact smallholding and carrying went well together: 'the man who procures a parcel of land from which to procure a livelihood finds that his team, however small it may be, is not fully employed, and he too begins to compete for the available employment for horses.'[9]

The transport needs of nineteenth and early-twentieth century Britain were met by a vast, and ever increasing, army of horse-drawn cabs, vans, carts and waggons. For while there is no doubt that the coming of the railways reduced the demand for long distance road haulage, it is also clear that it provided a vital stimulus to local traffic of all kinds. According to a recent estimate by Professor Thompson, the number of trade horses grew prodigiously from just over 150,000 in 1811, to 161,000 in 1851, 500,000 in 1891, and about 832,000 in 1911. The half million horse-drawn vehicles on the roads in 1891 provided employment for nearly 200,000 carmen, carriers, carters and hauliers. For the historian of penny capitalism, the difficulty of course is to decide what proportion of these workers engaged in the various branches of the road transport industry used their own horse and vehicle.[10]

Some tentative generalisation is possible. It appears that the small general carrier, the single man with his horse and cart, was able to retain a niche in road haulage. He could undertake all sorts of casual jobs: moving coal or furniture, manure or laundry, food or building materials, as the opportunity presented itself. Indeed to some extent the range of possibilities probably expanded during the second half of the century. There was goods and luggage to be taken to and from railway stations, football supporters to be taken to and from matches and, most important of all perhaps, contracts to be won with the new local authorities. By the 1880s 'the new Warwickshire County Council had taken the roads in hand. Hartshill stone was being applied on almost all of them . . . The stone brought new economic chances for some folk. Local men with a cart or two contracted to convey it from the railway yard and tip it beside the sections of road that were due for mending.'[11] For the ambitious, well organised — and conveniently situated — man, there was the additional possibility of running a regular carrying service: into the nearest town perhaps, calling at two or three villages on the way. From his survey of late-Victorian Leicestershire, Professor Everitt has shown that most village carriers were small, self-employed men with little capital, while some of the part-time carriers in the Leicester region 'were clearly of very humble status and were described simply as gardeners, cottagers or cowkeepers'.[12] So although it is impossible to quantify working-class involvement in the organisation of road haulage, what little evidence there is does suggest that the penny capitalist remained of some consequence throughout the nineteenth and early-twentieth centuries.

In the cab trade, on the other hand, opportunities for advancement tended to diminish as the nineteenth century wore on. The trade itself was under increasing threat. In London, for example, there was growing competition from the electric tram, the horse (and later the motor) bus, the motor taxi, the underground railway, the telegram and the telephone. 'We do get a few jobs through the telephone that we might not have got without it,' admitted the *Cab Trade Record*, 'But then it largely does away with the need for a cab at all. Take it this way now. There's lots of times a business man has some little matter to settle with one in another office. In the old style he would have got a cab and

gone over, or sent his clerk the same way. Now he just rings
up on the telephone, and it's done.'[13] Moreover within the
trade it was the self-employed owner-driver who was particularly vulnerable. There was increasing pressure from large
proprietors such as the Birmingham Cab Company which,
within a year of its foundation, was able to boast of 282 cabs,
fifty four cars and forty one other vehicles. These large firms
were then able to squeeze the small man. In Dundee, for
example, the wealthier proprietors made life difficult for
their competitors in 1886 by halving their fares from a shilling
to sixpence for all trips within half a mile of the railway
stations and steamboat piers. The reduced opportunities in
the cab trade are illustrated by the fact that the only two
late-nineteenth-century London owner-drivers whose backgrounds it has been possible to identify both emerged not
from ordinary working class jobs, but from 'good service'.
Opportunities did not disappear completely however. The
rules of the Amalgamated Cab Drivers' Society continued to
include the specific provision that any driver who managed to
save up enough to buy an old 'lot' should be allowed to
remain a member although he would be debarred from any
further voice in the management of the society.[14]

It is no easier to discover the profits made by self-employed
and often part-time carters and cab drivers than it is for most
of the other penny capitalists considered in this book. Yet it
is clear that the owner-driver faced serious, and in some cases
mounting, difficulties. His investment was at constant risk:
cabs and carts were sometimes stolen while any horse was a
perpetual worry. It was never easy to obtain a reliable animal.
Horse dealers were notorious for their dishonesty: they 'were
all rogues. They'd warrant it [was broken], as long as they
got their sovereigns and got rid of their horse, they were
landed.'[15] Fellow drivers were often no better: in 1884 a
small cab proprietor from the Brompton district of London
sued another for £4 15s. because the mare which he had
bought turned out to have glanders and had to be destroyed.
This could be a catastrophe from which a small man never
recovered. Alexander Somerville recalls his father's efforts to
attain independence early in the nineteenth century:

My father settled in the town of Alloa, on the Firth of

Forth, when a young man. He had a horse and cart, and carted coals or lime, or such things, for hire. His horse had the common equine name of Dick and was very much respected by his owner. But Dick took ill and died, and left that owner too poor to buy another. So Dick's hide, and the cart, and the harness, were sold, and your grandfather went to work as a labourer at the great lime works of the Earl of Elgin, near Dunfermline, whither his elder brother had preceded him.[16]

Feeding and stabling were a constant drain of income. By the 1880s, for instance, a stable with two or three stalls in the Kings Cross district of London cost about six shillings a week. Grazing could be had on the roadside in some country districts, but by the turn of the century it was said to cost about ten shillings a week to feed a town horse. So by this time it could take fifteen shillings per week simply to keep the horse, fifteen shillings which had to be recouped before any profit at all could be shown.[17]

The prosperity of hauliers and cab drivers alike depended upon the weather: the former suffered in bad weather; the latter in good. The mild January of 1902, for instance, 'was the means of nearly all the cabs being on the streets, instead of them being packed up in the yards, so that the competition for the small demand was very keen, and cabby came off at the finish very badly'.[18] Cab drivers, it has already been seen, came under increasing pressure during the final quarter of the nineteenth century. The trade press was full of complaints against overcompetition, police harassment, and the 'rotten privilege system' (whereby each cab was licensed to ply from one stand only, and that probably a poor one since the better ones tended to be monopolised by the large proprietors). Overcompetition, it has been shown over and over again, was the bane of all forms of penny capitalism. It was certainly the ruin of many owner-drivers trying to make their way in the road transport industry. As early as 1826 a Lancashire coal-owner explained the problems of 'The Farmers and many that are not exactly Farmers' who transported coal from Prescot to Liverpool: 'they are Poor Fellows who have one horse carts, and if they cannot get Five Shillings a day with that one Horse, they are obliged to get Four Shillings or what they can.'[19] Overcompetition stifled initiative. 'The cab driver who could look forward to some day being able to become the owner of a vehicle and horses of his own – not, as at present [1886], in streets overstocked with cabs – would have a great inducement to thrift.'[20]

Confronted by so many difficulties, it is hardly surprising that some self-employed drivers and carriers failed to earn an adequate income, let alone to accumulate capital. It was particularly hard to make satisfactory provision for old age. Thus in 1884 the 240 members of the London 'Hackney Carriage Mutual Benefit Society – Small Proprietory' were supporting twenty-three 'worn-out' drivers and in 1902 the *Cab Trade Record* gave considerable publicity to the trade union benefit being organised for Bill Johnson, a loyal union member, who had suffered the misfortune of losing four horses in a single week.[21] Yet profits were made from the movement of goods. Persistence was needed to succeed against established competition. At Tysoe in Warwickshire, seventeen-year-old Arthur Ashby

worked on his reluctant father to let him start a coal business. Hitherto customers had trundled their wheelbarrows to the dealers or hired a horse and cart to fetch coal from Banbury; but Arthur would deliver to their doors and charge them fourteen instead of fifteen pence the hundredweight! The boys liked the driving to and fro that the business involved, but there was also much heavy lifting, from the railway truck to the cart at Kineton, from the cart to the stock at home. Then it was sacked, weighed and lifted to the trolley again, all by two boys. The girls wondered to see the tough strength of the fifteen-year-old Dick, lifting the sacks of coal. But the boys' work grew slack when the fires died down in summer and there was a new problem; the horses they had bought could not 'eat off their heads in idleness'. The brothers' next idea was to haul stones for road-making. A Dutch auction for carrying stone for various lengths of road in the district was to be held at Brailes . . . The older hauliers were accustomed to divide the work among them, arranging prices beforehand, and were annoyed at the youngsters' irruption. In the end, the boys took one section of the road at a price which meant that a horse, 'man', and cart earned one shilling and threepence per day . . . However, the boys had learned one lesson and their fellow hauliers another. Next year they were invited into the little ring.[22]

It is impossible to judge the typicality of such an enterprise. It does seem reasonable to assume, however, that in the road haulage industry, as in other sectors of the economy, the survival of so many small concerns meant that they were able to provide their organisers with at least some sort of income.

The profitability of passenger traffic is marginally better documented. Cabmen did their best to counteract their high costs and the burden of 'cab-bilkers' who left without paying, by over-charging whenever this was unlikely to be detected. Moreover, bad weather and, in London, special events like the Boat Race, the Smithfield Show and the Great Exhibition of 1851, were all good for business. Frank Kemsley's horse-dealer father was perhaps typical of successful one-man carriers. Based near Ashford in Kent, he gradually built up a useful part-time business: passengers hired him for weddings and for journeys to the local railway station while 'the old parson always used to get us to take him out to some other parson's house to tea, lunch and that and I, I used to drive him dress myself up and drive him there and perhaps earn 10 bob.'[23] Thus the impression gained from a consideration of penny capitalist endeavour in road transport would seem to confirm the view that people were 'the best paying cargo of all.'[24]

There is no doubt that the transport system as a whole underwent profound and well-documented changes during the course of the nineteenth and early-twentieth centuries. But this should not be allowed to obscure the stubborn persistence of many old-established techniques and methods of organisation, particularly at the local level. Short distance road traffic, both freight and passenger, continued to be organised much as it had been in the seventeenth century; it 'was characterized by individual or small partnership enter-prise, often with single carriers operating regular services on a co-operative basis'.[25]

7

Entertainment

Popular entertainment was another old-established service which continued to be provided by a small but persistent band of working-class entrepreneurs. Again, however, the sources are elusive and it is not always easy to distinguish between employees and those actually owning the means of production. One worker-capitalist who did own his means of production was the street-entertainer, still today a popular figure in public imagination. Yet from mid-century, if not before, the penny capitalist street-entertainer faced growing problems not only from public disapproval and from police harassment but from the increasing capitalisation of the entertainment industry itself. Well known is Mayhew's Punch and Judy man who, when he bought his equipment for 35s. in the mid 1830s was able, with his partner, to earn two or three pounds a day. By the time he met Mayhew, he was struggling to make any sort of living at all.[1]

It would be a mistake to exaggerate the decline of street-entertaining however. For while growing urbanisation, increasing leisure time, and rising real incomes all encouraged the substantial entrepreneurs of popular culture, they also provided new opportunities for even the smallest part-time penny capitalist. It is simply not true to suggest that by the 1870s 'The only successful street showmen were those with some modern technology — a telescope or a camera: the others were being obliterated by competition.'[2] The ownership and exploitation of animals remained widespread. The 'happy family', whereby a group of animals such as cats, rats and pigeons were displayed together, was inaugurated by a Coventry stocking-weaver in the mid 1840s. By the end of the following decade the practice had spread to London where one exhibitor told Mayhew that it cost 12*s.* a week to keep his fifty four animals and that his takings varied between eight and thirty shillings. Other performing animals were displayed right up to the end of the century. In the spring of 1890, for example, two Italians, claiming to be agricultural labourers, were prosecuted for allowing their performing bear to cause an obstruction to the Estcourt Road in Fulham. Nor, given the publicity recently afforded to the 'elephant man', is it possible to overlook the continuing popularity of freak shows. Thus in February 1890 Charles Taylor rented a butcher's shop on the Stoke Newington Road in north London, hung a twelve feet by ten feet painting of his wife across the front, played an organ and trumpet and charged members of the public a penny to see his wife, Madame Howard the 'African Lion-Faced Lady'.[3] Traditional mechanical devices such as weighing machines and barrel organs also remained popular throughout the period. Even in the present century a weighing chair could be had for 30*s.* and a barrel organ hired or bought relatively cheaply. The trade press carried advertisements for second-hand, trunk-mounted piano organs able to play ten of the latest tunes for sale for as little as ten pounds. The result was that in Edwardian Preston for example, 'A chap with one leg used to come. He used to go down one street with a barrel-organ and he would play hymns and if he didn't get anything he would go in the next street and he would play Catholic tunes, like "Faith of our Fathers". Then he would go back on C of E music.'[4]

It is true, however, that street-entertainers willing and able to seize the opportunities afforded by the new technology might hope to reap substantial dividends. By mid-century a good microscope could be bought for ten pounds, a complete set of photographic apparatus for half that sum and a second-hand peep show for as little as £2 10*s.*. In London, Mayhew noticed, photographic portraits were becoming a regular item of street commerce. Microscope and telescope exhibitors could expect to recoup their outlay within a year at most. Mayhew interviewed a tailor who took out his eighty-pound telescope after work, charged a penny a peep and made between 2*s.* 6*d.* and a pound an evening. He did even better on special occasions such as the eclipse of the moon (in

October 1856) or the sailing of the fleet (when he took his telescope to Portsmouth). Takings averaged, he estimated, £125 a year. Other optical equipment came onto the market towards the end of the century. By 1900 a penny-in-the-slot kalloscop, complete with lamp and eighteen pictures, could be bought for 35s.; a new cinematograph (or bioscope) could be obtained for £18; while for £21 10s. the would-be entrepreneur could purchase a street machine capable of showing twenty foot pictures – the 'Greatest Money-taker', it was claimed, 'of the Nineteenth Century'.[5] There were various ways of increasing the takings. When on tour, one bioscope proprietor used to cut up old films into short lengths which he sold as souvenirs for a penny each at the end of the performance.[6] But it was not easy for even the most astute to perceive the full potential of the new medium. A Lancaster man recalls that well before the First World War, 'a chap lived next door to me, a retired actor . . . and pictures were just coming and he wanted me to go in with him and I could be the operator. You could get two changes of pictures a week at an offer of seven pounds ten. You hired them from the manufacturers and I said to him, "Oh, it'll fizzle out in all time," and he said, "You'll see," and I have seen.'[7]

Nor is it possible to maintain that penny capitalists were completely squeezed out of the fairgrounds by their mid-century revival on the basis of new technology and increased investment. Naturally the latest fairground machinery, such as the £275 steam roundabout advertised for sale in 1900 ('A gold mine to anyone with a small capital'), was far beyond the reach of the penny capitalist showman. Yet the small man did retain a niche in the world of entertainment. Arthur Harding remembers one of his neighbours in the East End of London.

> He had a round-about, all gaily painted, with little flags flying. There were about six seats. You'd get five minutes for a halfpenny a time. There were little chairs and he used to spin it round himself - he didn't have no mechanical controls. A donkey would pull it along when he took it to fairs, but it didn't do anything else. He'd put the kids on – or the mothers – and then he'd spin it round. 'Course he didn't charge a halfpenny a time when he went over

Hampstead Heath, he charged twopence or threepence then.[8]

Thus the penny capitalist street-entertainer was threatened, though not destroyed, by the late-nineteenth-century expansion and capitalisation of the leisure industry. In the conurbations and the emerging seaside resorts in particular there survived a large, if indeterminate, number of full and part-time independent entertainers. 'In truth,' observed a special correspondent to one of the trade papers at the beginning of this century, 'there is a real nomadic, or itinerant profession of performers quite exclusive from the real stage, of which we seem to have no record since the days when the Brothers Mayhew issued their "London Labour and the Poor".'[9]

Other workers continued to provide entertainment indoors. Those blessed with both musical and entrepreneurial skills sometimes organised dances. In early-twentieth-century Barrow-in-Furness, for example, a joiner at the giant Vickers works played the violin, ran his own dance band and arranged dances: small ones at the local baths, larger ones in the Town Hall. He played only old-fashioned dances such as waltzes, lancers, veletas and quadrilles and 'was most strict, terrible, they had to dance so far apart. He wouldn't let them dance cheek to cheek.'[10]

Such prudery was unusual among penny capitalist entertainers who were more likely to seek to profit from sexual enjoyment than to try to inhibit it. The control of prostitution is supposed to represent, of course, one classic avenue of working-class escape. Naturally the discussion of any aspect of nineteenth and early-twentieth-century prostitution is beset with difficulties, and none more so than the question of working-class involvement in brothel-keeping. While Mayhew was right to define brothels as 'houses where speculators board, dress, and feed women, living upon the farm of their persons', it is never easy to identify brothel-keepers, let alone to discover their class. Naturally brothel-owners never described themselves as such in the census, and it is difficult to distinguish them from those running 'accommodation' or 'receiving' houses, in which prostitutes rented rooms to transact their business.[11]

Although it is impossible to assess precisely the number of

working-class brothel-keepers, they were always common especially in dockyard areas and in garrison towns. Mayhew found for example that in working-class districts of London such as Shadwell, Spitalfields and Whitechapel, brothel-keeping was 'a favourite mode of investing money'.[12] Moreover it seems that in late-nineteenth-century York a number of retired prostitutes themselves managed to organise 'two or three low-class whores in a common lodging-house or cottage of ill repute'. Thus in the summer of 1864 a twenty-three-year-old, syphilitic prostitute, Elizabeth Hough, applied to the Guardians for relief. Just four years later she was charged with 'permitting persons of opposite sexes to sleep in the same room of her lodging-house'.[13] It was common too for publicans and beer-shop keepers, many of whom were penny capitalists, to run their own brothels. Thus in the early 1830s at Fernley in Lancashire one beer-house keeper with four spare rooms used to charge his customers 2*d*. for a quart of ale — or a shilling if they wanted a girl to go with it. At the end of the following decade it was claimed that well over a tenth of the publicans and beer-shop keepers in Blackburn either harboured prostitutes or maintained auxiliary brothels.[14]

Still further evidence of working-class involvement may be derived from an examination of the occupations claimed by prosecuted brothel-owners. Great caution is obviously necessary but it does seem reasonable to assume that the claims represent the accused's previous occupations or at least provide some indication of the social class to which they belonged. In York, for instance, it has been possible to identify four husband and wife brothel-keeping teams active between 1838 and 1877: the husbands claimed employment as a joiner, a housepainter, a lodging-house keeper and an agricultural labourer. By far the most valuable insight into the occupational backgrounds of mid-nineteenth-century brothel-keepers is provided by Mayhew's analysis of the 143 people arrested for keeping 'common brothels' in the metropolis between 1850 and 1860. Sixty of the 143 claimed other occupations and of these thirty nine (sixty five per cent) were clearly working class: thirteen servants, one sawyer, three laundresses, nine labourers, two smiths, six carpenters, two painters and three bricklayers. A further fourteen (twenty three per cent) were apparently of working-class background: one sailor, three tailors, one printer, one cabinetmaker, one brassfounder, one carver and gilder, two watchmakers and four shoemakers.[15]

Brothel-keeping was potentially very profitable. Of course, police hostility posed an increasing, if inconsistent, hazard. The intensity of official regulation varied considerably: enforcement tended to be strict in the period preceding the annual Brewster sessions but always seemed to be lax in large, sprawling port cities such as London and Liverpool. Whatever the difficulties, they seem to have been more than offset by the financial opportunities which brothel-keeping offered. As well as charging rent for each prostitute's room and claiming a percentage (or even the whole) of her earnings, the brothel-keeper could sell drinks and supplement his income by robbing the girls' clients.[16]

Another lucrative, if equally unacceptable, service performed by working men and women was the provision of gambling and betting facilities. Informal gaming among friends and acquaintances maintained its popularity until the end of the period and beyond. Arthur Harding can remember from the beginning of this century a neighbour who 'was a docker at the Surrey docks and when work was scarce he would play, or rather run, a "Crown and Anchor" board [a kind of roulette played with a board and counters] at the docks'.[17] Others ran illegal gambling clubs. In 1910, for example, a London tailor, Morris Cohen, was fined twenty pounds plus three guineas costs for using a flat in Newport Buildings, Soho for unlawful gaming.[18]

Bookmaking, unlike brothel-keeping, expanded dramatically during the final quarter of the nineteenth century. Alongside casual, informal gambling, there emerged a formal and increasingly capitalised mass betting industry based upon horse racing. This expansion offered ambitious workmen all sorts of new opportunities on the fringes of the bookmaking world: as tipsters, as touts or agents who collected the bets, as 'scouts' or 'watchers' who kept a lookout for the police, or as 'runners' who carried the betting slips from the tout to the bookmaker. To such men the transition to bookmaking must have appeared highly attractive. At the same time even the dimmest punter could presumably see that there was more money to be made from bookmaking than there ever was from betting. Indeed, according to George Bernard Shaw, 'nearly everybody whose social rank does not exclude such an occupation would be a bookmaker if he could'.[19] Most bookmakers probably began their careers by organising sweepstakes on big races like the 'Oaks' or the 'Derby', going on perhaps to run a regular 'book' during their lunch hour. The transition to bookmaking proper was eased from the 1880s onwards by the introduction of 'S P' (starting price) betting. By using the starting prices which were beginning to be listed in the *Sporting Life* and other newspapers, the novice bookmaker avoided the difficult job of compiling his own odds and reassured customers that his odds were fair. As a result, it seems, more and more working people took to bookmaking as their chief source of income. In the East End of London, for example, there emerged a distinct group of small 'kerb-stone' bookmakers who, as their name implied, conducted the whole of their business in the streets.[20]

Despite the legendary profitability of bookmaking, it was not easy to establish a successful business. Violence, and the threat of violence, was never far away. The small bookmaker was a soft target.

> People would say, 'Go along to the racecourses, you'll get a few quid, everybody wants to see you.' You'd go with a racing tout and he'd introduce you to the different bookies and say 'You know so and so' and he'd mention your name and the bookmaker would look at you and he'd give you a couple of quid in the hat.[21]

The uncertain state of the law was even more of a problem. Between 1853 and 1906 cash bookmaking was legal in specified clubs and enclosures, but not in pubs or on the streets. The difficulty was exacerbated by the local bye-laws against obstruction which were passed around the turn of the century and it was not until 1906 that it was finally decided that two people did not constitute an assembly under the Betting Act. After 1906 the law was perfectly clear: all off-course betting was illegal. In fact, it was even claimed that it was the hostility of the Middlesborough police towards street betting which encouraged at least one workman to start taking bets himself in the mill where he worked.[22]

According to a recent commentator, 'Mass betting was the most successful example of working-class self-help in the modern era.'[23] Certainly there can be no doubt that book-makers were nearly always working class, no doubt either that they could make a reasonable living particularly if they were careful to accept only small bets when first starting. There were many successful worker bookmakers. A Leeds engineer-ing worker left the firm of F W Tannett-Walker to become 'rather a prosperous bookmaker', earning more money, his employer admitted, than he would have done had he stayed on to become a foreman in the works.[24] In Edinburgh a twenty-year-old apprentice cooper, Robert Spittal, started a football pool in 1902. Competitors had to forecast the result and the number of goals scored by each team in six Scottish football matches. He printed the coupons in his own house, sold them for twopence each and awarded a first prize of two guineas. This part-time business expanded and prospered un-til 1923 when its organiser decided to bring it to an end.[25] Working-class bookmakers were both typical and untypical of other penny capitalists: untypical in that they could reason-ably hope to earn substantial profits; typical in that it was hard for them to exorcise their working-class identity. Book-making's lack of respectability prevented its practitioners from moving out of their class. 'Bookmakers, then, particularly illegal bookmakers, had little more respectability than do pornographers today.'[26]

The increasing capitalisation and commercialisation of the leisure industry did not prevent penny capitalist providers of popular entertainment from maintaining an important niche in the market. Although street-entertainers were under increas-ing challenge during the second half of the nineteenth century, there is no reason to suspect any significant diminution of working-class brothel-keeping and every reason to identify a substantial increase in working-class bookmaking.

8

Personal Services

There is no reason to suppose that the demand for personal services dwindled before the advance of industrialisation and urbanisation. Of all the many tasks performed by working men and women, the most promising were those, like washing and hairdressing, which could be started by the mere provision of labour but which could be developed until they became true penny capitalist enterprises. In fact part-time laundry work was always the most common way for working-class women to try to earn extra income to protect their existing standard of living. Often it was the first resort of the bereaved and the deserted. Most women simply went out to wash in the homes of local middle and upper-class families, but those with ambition (or more prosaically with young children) probably preferred to work in their own homes. The minimum equipment needed to take in washing was a tub or boiler, a dolly, a mangle and an iron. Those fortunate enough to possess a little capital (provided, perhaps, following bereavement) were well placed to set up on their own. Widows of Fife miners killed in the pit were sometimes provided by the coalowners with 'a large mangle' so that their 'customers and neighbours could get their washing mangled at so much a bundle'.[1] Other sources of capital included the collections commonly made at work or in the street where the deceased had lived. In pre-World War I Preston 'If a woman's husband died they used to buy a mangle, if she was hard up, and had a big family, so she could earn a living doing washing for other people.'[2] On rare occasions the bereaved even received sufficient money to purchase the stock and goodwill of a small, established, full-time laundry or mangling business. But these were the exceptions. Most women did not enjoy even these modest financial advantages. A girl brought up at Nelson in Lancashire remembers that when her mother first began to take in washing, she had to wring it out by hand. It was only by saving the little money which she earned that she was able to invest in a second-hand wringer.[3]

By one means or another a surprisingly large number of women did manage to acquire the necessary equipment. Typical of so many was Bernie Baker's neighbour at Shorne in Kent who 'got her living by doing peoples mangling, and the mangles they stretched along a big room she had . . . Then she did it all day, every day, for different people.'[4] Impressionistic evidence suggests that this was not uncommon; that every working-class street had its self-employed, part-time penny capitalist washer-woman or mangler, and that many streets had several. This is confirmed by the statistical evidence. For although contemporary social surveys and recent oral investigations examine only a minute sample of the late-nineteenth and early-twentieth-century working class, the evidence which they present has proved to be remarkably consistent. When Arnold Freeman published his study of seventy one Birmingham boy workers in 1914, he revealed that of their sixty six mothers, three (4.6 per cent) were taking in washing. Similarly, the oral study of working-class Barrow-in-Furness and Lancaster between 1890 and 1914 shows that at least three of the seventy five respondents' mothers (four per cent) took in washing on a part-time basis — none of whom, significantly, find any mention at all in the census returns.[5]

Some families depended upon laundry work as their chief source of income. By 1871 about seven per cent of the family heads in Kensal New Town in Kensington were laundrymen, serving the nearby, expanding, fashionable districts of Bayswater and Belgravia. Each of these husband and wife businesses employed about six laundresses, ironers and manglers and sometimes a child to pick up and deliver the washing. They 'represented the closest the village had to an entrepreneurial class' and gave Kensal New Town the nickname of 'Soap-Suds Island'.[6] Even the census could not overlook full-time penny capitalism on this scale. The returns show that by 1911 more than forty per cent of all home-based, female washers, ironers and manglers were self-employed. So towards the end of the period between four and five per cent of working class women were taking in washing or mangling during their supposedly spare time. This figure might rise appreciably in response to local middle-class demand: as laundries grew in size in these districts, so they tended to involve the husband and children and to become the families' major means of support.[7]

Oral testimony resounds to the horror of home laundering. The washing had to be collected (probably by the children), the boiler had to be filled, the coal collected, and the fire lit. The clothes had to be rinsed and 'dolleyed', mangled, ironed and finally returned to the customer. It was all hard, physical labour which had to be squeezed in between (or around) all the usual household chores. The difficulty of drying washing in the British climate led inevitably to arguments with neighbours and, not least, with other members of the family. The daughter of a Lancaster painter and decorator recalls how she and her mother were scared to have the washing drying round the fire when her father arrived home: 'I used to hurry up and get them washed and dried and ironed and back at night.'[8] A successful laundry could reverse the sexual roles within a marriage. A Kent woman remembers how her mother took her revenge on her husband during the First World War. She began to take in washing from soldiers and 'bought seven plots of land with that money, she thought I won't let him have it for booze, I'm going to buy something with this'.[9] Many years earlier one Portsmouth mangle-woman had completed the household form in the 1851 census: she placed her own name in the space reserved for the head of the household while in the dependants' column she wrote, 'John — husband, turns my mangle'.[10]

The punishing schedule of home washing sometimes proved too great a burden. The son of a widowed Kent woman remembers that his mother

had an ambition that she could open a laundry, a private do. They'd go round and collect, her and a widow she knew, elderly widow, who was living with her son. She and this widow went into partnership, she'd come over and work at our house, and between them they'd go round and collect washing from the big houses, wash it and take it back you see. Do it all theirselves. Private. Well she done it, but the woman, this widow, let her down you know, she didn't come sometimes. Mother got behind a little, then people stopped, it was a failure. So that's why it only lasted about a year.[11]

Even if such disasters were avoided, taking in washing was not likely to result in very high earnings. By the early years of this century charges seem to have stabilised: washing and ironing, 2s. 6d. a bundle (including powder); mangling, 1d. per dozen items. Even women who took in sufficient washing to be able to employ assistants did not earn a great deal. In the Wiltshire village of Corsley, for example,

The prices charged for washing are not uniform, but most charge at a low rate, leaving a very small margin of profit. A laundress whose gross earnings are 12s. weekly has to pay a woman for two days' work and provide her food. She must provide materials such as soap, and extra firing, which amounts to something considerable in damp weather. If 3s. be allowed for the extra labour and 1s. 6d. for firing and materials, her nett (*sic*) earnings are 7s. 6d.[12]

Of course even earnings as low as these could be of vital importance to a hard-pressed working-class family. The daughter of a Barrow moulder insists upon the value of such income: 'A lot of the labourers' wives took in washing to keep the children up to form. Ther's a lot of people that I know now could have been in rags and tatlers but weren't.'[13] Moreover there was one other important way in which it was possible to derive advantage from any laundry business, however small. 'The washing of clothes provided a regular and readily pawnable commodity.'[14] Naturally for most of the century it is possible to trace the practice only when it was discovered and prosecuted. It was of long standing however. In 1840, for instance, a Liverpool woman pledged the washing belonging to the mate of a ship at five different pawn-shops; while in London the elderly Susannah Bailey raised five pounds on the sheets, tablecloths and other linen belonging to a customer from Westminster. Clearly, however, such prosecutions were but the tiny tip of a very large iceberg.[15]

If the organisation of small, generally part-time laundries was one service which retained its popularity with working-class women, the provision of accommodation was another. In both cases motives were mixed. A few women saw taking in lodgers as the first step towards financial security, but most viewed it as a means of supplementing their income, as part of the struggle to preserve rather than to improve their existing standard of living. The capital requirements were small: the use of a spare room, a few extra sheets and some spare crockery. Some landladies had little choice in the matter for it was not uncommon for miners and farm-workers living in tied accommodation to be required to take in lodgers. Otherwise it was normal practice for middle-aged women and those with young children to take advantage of any demand created by local industrial or recreational development. Fred Kitchen remembers that 'the coming of the railroad did a certain amount of good' to his south Yorkshire village:

> the village was much frequented by tourists, and nearly every cottage bore the card: 'Teas Provided'. Well, Little Norwood took down its cards with 'Teas Provided' and put up other cards bearing the inscription, 'Lodgings', and every one with a spare bed, and many who hadn't a bed worth mentioning, went in for lodgers. It was the gold rush for Little Norwood, never before had it seen so many golden sovereigns waiting to be picked up, and it made the most of its chances.[16]

But it was in the new coastal resorts that penny capitalism made its greatest contribution as working-class women responded to the opportunities created by changing patterns of leisure. So whereas in 1871 most of the four hundred landladies in Blackpool had catered for middle-class families, in 1911 the vast majority of the town's four thousand landladies were entertaining working-class visitors. Thus over the country the number of families taking in lodgers tended to vary widely: from as low as four per cent in late-nineteenth-century Barrow and Lancaster, to twenty three per cent in mid-century Preston, to as high as thirty three per cent in early-twentieth-century Middlesborough.[17]

Charges were low. In mid-nineteenth-century Preston single lodgers were charged from 9*d*. to 2*s*. 6*d*. a week depending on the facilities provided. By the turn of the century land-

ladies in Blackpool and elsewhere were charging a shilling
per person per night, although some were beginning to offer
a double bed for one and sixpence. In the coalfields the
standard charge for board and lodging (including washing)
had stabilised at between twelve and fifteen shillings a week.
Although, as in other forms of penny capitalism, income was
most assured where ambitions were most modest, families
providing accommodation in their homes could not possibly
make large sums of money. Thus it was said at the beginning
of this century that of the twelve to fifteen shillings a week
which lodgers paid in County Durham, some two or three
shillings was supposed to be profit. But for such small sums,
a heavy price might have to be paid. Even when the lodger
was quiet, temperate, good-natured and 'pretty careful with
the furniture', he could still drive the family to distraction:
'sure as ever we've got a bit of something nice and hot, there
he'll stick, and he'll sniff and he'll sniff, and stare, and pass
remarks, and sigh, till one or the other of us – and I must
own it's oftenest me – will say, "Like a bit?" and then,
without no more asking than you'd give a dog, he pegs into
it until what I meant for next day's dinner looks pretty
foolish.'[18] Just occasionally, however, the landlady could
do really well. The daughter of a Lancaster painter and
decorator remembers that 'An old lady down where we
lived she'd all sort of lodgers. She had one that was a bit soft
and they called him same name as her and she used to look
after his bank book and when he died [early this century] of
course she got it. He had nobody you see.'[19]

Naturally it was much more difficult to obtain the use of a
bona fide lodging or boarding-house, and as a result these
tended to be acquired by middle-aged couples who had
managed to accumulate some sort of capital and wanted to
obtain independence of wage labour. Thus of the nearly
26,000 lodging and boarding-house keepers listed in the 1871
census, two-thirds were aged forty-five or above. The census
figures reveal too that their numbers more than kept pace with
the rise in population during the second half of the century,
increasing from 17,563 in 1851 (equal to one in every 462
of the adult population) to 49,508 (one in 445) in 1891. The
census figures reveal again a significant expansion in the newly

emerging seaside holiday resorts. Between 1871 and 1891 the number of boarding and lodging-house keepers in Brighton increased by more than twenty per cent, and by the beginning of this century the social origins of Blackpool lodging-house keepers were said to be 'unequivocally working-class'.[20]

Boarding and lodging-house keepers operated in one of three ways: some simply provided accommodation; some provided meals of their own choosing; but most cooked the food which their guests brought in. Whatever the system, it was hard work. In one Margate boarding house,

Daily routine would be up in the morning, they'd all want cups of tea. Round you'd go with a blimmin' tray of tea to every room. Then, if you'd got the sitting room, which we didn't, we had a sitting room but only one lot had the sitting room, it had the big bedroom, because it was a bigger family. The other rooms, they had to have their meals in their room. Well then you'd have to get their tray ready. And if they went out before breakfast you'd go up there perhaps have to empty slops, make the bed, lay the breakfast. Then you have the breakfast to cook and have that ready by the time they came in. You'd have to do that to the other rooms you see. Well then you have to wait for them to go out, then go collect all the trays, and then you've got the basement to do as well, and you had all those stairs to do. Then you'd go out with your broom, brush and dust pan and a duster, top of the house down, to each room, and the staircase all the way down. And if they were late, somebody else had got to start doing all the veg. You had to keep everybody's vegetables separate. You had to know whose vegetables they were. You couldn't cook everybody's greens together because they didn't perhaps all want greens. And perhaps somebody had got different potatoes you see. You'd to do all that separate. You can imagine the saucepans you had. Remember whose was who. Whose meat was who.You had to mark all that. Oh dear, it used to be a game. Then if there was puddings you had all those to do. And then some would say can we have a cup of tea after dinner, and if the old girl was in a good mood she might say yes. But if she didn't feel energetic with these sort of people she'd say I'm sorry I haven't got time. Then she'd get the dinner things all done, then you'd got to go round clearing all up and tidying up again, and lay the tea. And perhaps the old girl would say, well I think I'd better start and do my washing. Because you keep having washing all the time to do. So she'd have to start her washing. And after tea it was clear away again, go round and empty all slops and fill all up again. Turn the beds down. Then some would have cheek enough to want suppers. They wouldn't be satisfied with just bread and cheese, they'd probably want anything else, and cook that. If they wanted fish and chips or anything they had to bring that in on their own. But it was blinkin' hard work.[21]

Whatever the system, the object of course was to make money. But boarding and lodging-house keepers could not charge high prices if they were to retain their working-class clientele. Visitors early this century to a Lytham boarding-house were charged four shillings per bed per night (and only allowed to squeeze two people into each bed). Meanwhile at Margate one penny capitalist boarding-house keeper charged two shillings for bed and breakfast and 25s. a week for a room (or 30s. if the family was exceptionally large). Given such low charges, proprietors did all they could to augment their incomes. Since it was usually counter-productive to cut the guests' standard of living directly, efforts were made to accommodate as many visitors as possible, to employ only members of the family, and to minimise the cost of advertising by relying on personal recommendations supplemented by a notice in the front window.[22]

The profitability of holiday lodging and boarding-houses was precarious. Competition could be fierce, demand uncertain, the rent too high, and the season too short. There was the ever present risk of breakages, thefts and moonlight flits and the constant threat to domestic harmony by the reversal of family roles. Success was not unknown of course. The abstemious William Cartledge came to Blackpool from Derbyshire where he had worked as a coal miner and as an agricultural labourer. During his first five winters in a back-street lodging-house he was forced to work as a builder's labourer in order to make ends meet. Eventually, however, he obtained superior, sea-front premises, entered local politics and became mayor in 1914. Generally however it remained hard to earn a living without a reliable second source of income. In Blackpool at least it seems that those who struggled outnumbered those who prospered. One Margate boarding-house keeper was only too realistic: 'She always reckoned her letting was her firing and gas and lights and things like that.'[23]

To many working-class women providing accommodation or taking in washing seemed ideal ways of supplementing the family income. These enterprises were cheap to start and could be integrated (somehow) into the domestic routine. Yet for the ambitious they held out the hope at least of some financial, and perhaps even social, advance. Consequently these two surrogate family services constituted by far the most common form of female penny capitalism.

Yet there were others. Teaching was one: some working women ran dancing classes while others found themselves able to give up ordinary work and make a living from teaching the piano.[24] Indeed elementary school teaching has long been recognised as one of the few avenues of upward mobility accessible to the nineteenth-century working-class girl. Accordingly a good deal of research has been directed towards the recruitment, training and rewards of the ever-growing band of salaried elementary school teachers. By contrast, virtually nothing is known about those working people who founded and worked in their own private, profit orientated schools. Their so-called dame schools have been either ignored or denigrated: ignored because of lack of evidence; denigrated because what evidence does exist seems merely to reinforce the still powerful Whig view of educational history. The dame schools have been castigated for the poor quality of their staff, their modest aspirations, severe discipline, inadequate accommodation, restricted curriculum, long hours and general educational inefficiency.[25]

None of this, of course, diminishes the interest of dame schools to the historian of penny capitalism. Rather the reverse; for it was precisely these educational deficiencies which brought them within the reach of ordinary working people. The capital requirements were minimal: the use of a room, some teaching aids and a notice to hang in the window.

For example within a few months of his discharge from the
Royal Navy in 1816, William Brown found himself destitute
at a small village in Yorkshire. He hired a small room and
placed a notice in the window announcing 'a Day School by
William Brown'.

> I lay on a chaff bed on the floor having no bedstead; I
> had a board by the side and another at the bottom to pre-
> vent my rolling off. I got some sticks and boring some
> holes in the boards they served for forms by day, and find-
> ing a piece of broken spoon it served as a pencil, one of
> the form legs supplying the want of a ruler. I soon got
> scholars to the number of sixteen.[26]

This was unusual only in that the founder was a man. Schools
were opened by working women of all types, most often it
seems by the weak of the local community: the widowed, the
sick, the injured and occasionally the victimised. Illiteracy was
no barrier. When Horace Mann was conducting the Education
Census in 1851, he found that about five per cent of those
returning their forms from dame schools signed with a mark
(but then so did 0.2 per cent of public school teachers). Private school teachers, regretted the commissioners who were
examining English popular education in 1861, 'have rarely
been in any way trained to their profession, and they have
almost always selected it, either because they have failed in
other pursuits, or because, as in the case of widows, they have
been unexpectedly left in a state of destitution'.[27]

While it is generally acknowledged that dame schools were
of considerable importance during the early years of the
nineteenth century, it is commonly held that they quickly
withered away before the advance of superior, voluntary
education. Certainly there can be no doubt that dame schools
were very numerous at the beginning of the century — one
1819 estimate put their number at over three thousand in
urban areas alone. Thereafter the number of dame schools
increased rather than diminished. In fact, one recent commentator believes that the 1840s witnessed the 'efflorescence'
of dame and common day schools (catering for the under
sixes and the over sixes respectively).[28] Thus the Education
Census of 1851 revealed that England still had 13,495

'inferior' private schools (most of them dame schools) dealing with a third of all the children in school.[29]

It is all the more striking that this expansion should have taken place during precisely the same period that the voluntary agencies were making their greatest efforts (by 1861 practically a fifth of all children between the ages of three and six were attending public elementary schools). One explanation of this apparent paradox lies of course in the rapidly rising school age population. But equally important was the very spread of voluntary schools, for they were viewed in many working-class homes with the very deepest distrust. So when that pioneer of voluntary infant education, Samuel Wilderspin, played games with the children in order to ease their entry into his Spitalfields school, many were taken away, their mothers believing that they were not 'learning their lessons' and that it would be better to 'send them to Mrs So and So, where for 4d. a week they will learn something'.[30] Nor did the 1870 Education Act and subsequent legislation remove working-class distrust and bring about the immediate demise of this independent sector. The convenience of the local dame school, open all day but not too strict about regular attendance, apparently suited some mothers better than the new board schools. Indeed it was not unknown for even magistrates to connive with recalcitrant parents to evade the new attendance bye-laws. It could be said as late as 1881 that in the Bromsgrove district of Worcestershire, 'a fertile source of difficulty in enforcing bye-laws is to be found in the continued existence of private adventure schools . . . when a board begins to show vigour in carrying out its bye-laws, the dame school doors are freely open for the offenders'.[31] By this time, however, the working-class dame school was in decline, beaten down finally by growing competition from the board schools and by increasing government concern for health and the sanitary standards of school buildings. By the 1890s the dame school was virtually defunct.[32]

It is no easy matter to discover the profits which the working-class proprietors of dame schools were able to earn. Even gross income is hard to gauge. Fees ranged from twopence to sevenpence a week and roll sizes from one or two up to as many as thirty. At all events the income from fees alone can rarely have exceeded fifteen shillings a week; but there were ways of supplementing this basic income. The 1838 Select Committee on Education of the Poorer Classes was told that dame school proprietors 'often keep toy-shops and cake-shops, and they make something by the children, who buy their cakes'.[33]   Then in the lace-making and straw-plaiting districts of Devon, the South Midlands and East Anglia the 'craft' dame schools were more like workshops than schools. Even so, it is hardly surprising that few dame school proprietors were able to live without a second source of income. Schools opened and closed with monotonous regularity and even those which remained open were not necessarily very profitable. Thus in the early 1860s one seventy-year-old London widow explained that since the death of her husband twelve years before, her total weekly income amounted to 4s. 3d.: 2s. 6d. Poor Relief, supplemented by 1s. 9d. from her seven pupils. 'She complains of inability to buy meat, and without meat her strength fails.'[34]

The other personal services made available by penny capitalists were at once far less numerous and much more male dominated. The occasional eccentric provided his neighbours with bathing facilities. In 1858 it was reported from the small south Yorkshire mining village of Elsecar that 'a very intelligent working collier has fitted up a Turkish bath, in a very effective manner, and which is extensively patronised, nearly 200 colliers having enjoyed the Eastern luxury during the three weeks it has been in operation'.[35] Then during the coalmining boom of the early 1870s a miner living at West Cramlington in Northumberland converted his kitchen garden into a poultry farm and a cold shower which he was able to hire out. Even the ordinary domestic bath could be put to purposes other than those for which it was originally intended. A Kent woman lived next door to her village pub and when licensing hours were restricted during the First World War, she seized the opportunity presented by the presence of hop-pickers to hang out the fourteen to sixteen gallon galvanised baths in which she did her washing. When the pub closed after lunch the hop-pickers used to have a collection to pay 6d. (1s. 6d. at weekends) to hire the baths so that they could fill them with enough beer to keep them going until the pub re-opened at six o'clock.[36]

By far the most usual type of personal service provided by working men was the cutting of hair. In the countryside, in villages and in small towns haircutting long remained a part-time job, performed in the evenings or, more usually, on Sunday mornings. None of the small south Yorkshire villages which Fred Kitchen knew at the end of the century 'possessed a barber's shop — heads were too few for a barber to make a living out of them — so hair-cutting was a spare-time occupation reserved for Sunday morning. The shepherd was chief barber, though often a coachman or groom would set-up with horse clippers.'[37] Nor did it seem difficult, at least in the towns, to go full-time, to open a 'penny shaving shop'. Even at the beginning of this century the cost of converting a front room was not prohibitive: a basin could be bought for two shillings and a proper shaving chair for ten. Purpose-built premises too could be acquired relatively cheaply. In January 1910, for example, the *Hairdresser's Weekly Journal* was advertising for rent at 12s. 6d. a week a barber's shop and two rooms just four minutes from Westbourne Park station in west London. Indeed opening a small barber's must have seemed to offer all the advantages of running a shop with few of its disadvantages. Like the pub and beerhouse, the barber's was a place to meet friends and discuss the day's news. Like other forms of penny capitalism, it seemed to offer freedom: Walter Greenwood remembers his father — a supposedly full-time barber in Salford — trying 'without success, to convince my mother that his visits to the pub were "for the sake of business"'.[38] So easy was entry into the ranks of the employers (and so easy the descent back again) that hairdressing trade unions were forced to make provision both for members who became masters and for masters who were forced to give up their businesses. Not surprisingly, the established trade railed against the 'penny shaver', the 'lower class man, who, tired of the thraldom of assistantship, or perhaps he is a man who has never been an assistant at all, but who seeing that a couple or one Windsor chair, a pair of hair brushes, lather ditto, a shilling razor, and the indispensible "pole", is all that is required to start as "Professor" So-and-So, "Hairdresser", takes a front room which he is pleased to term a shop, and commences business. — Haircutting, 2d.,; "Easy" Shave, 1d.'[39]

As so often, neither the census returns nor local trade directories allow a reliable estimate to be made of the number of 'penny shaving shops' established by assistants and other workers. Nor do the available sources make it easy to determine the profitability of these small businesses. It is clear however that takings tended to be erratic. The busiest times were always Friday evenings and Sunday mornings and it was claimed that mid-century proposals to enforce Sunday closing 'would pauperize pretty well all the little common shaving shops in the country'.[40] But the tempo of the barber's week had changed little by the time Jack Hilton became a lather-boy in about 1909: 'I rather like the job. It had periods of slackness. And crikey! When it was busy, it was busy! The barber could swish a razor from ear to ear in one swoop, talk to three customers, and look through the window, all at the same time. On Friday nights, murderin' nights he called them, he took ten shillings in penny shaves and twopenny haircuts in a little over three hours.'[41] There were other benefits besides. Even small barbers often received complimentary tickets in exchange for advertising local cinema and theatrical performances. Nor can there be any doubt that barbers often doubled as bookmakers and drink sellers, particularly on Sunday mornings when pubs and beershops were closed.[42]

It is easy to exaggerate the success of part-time hairdressers. By the beginning of this century trade-union hostility was making it increasingly difficult for those outside the trade to cut hair in their spare time. So although the Rochdale Card and Blowing Room Association found itself unable to prevent one of its members from shaving and cutting hair in the evenings at 'under rates', it was decided in 1910 to take the matter to the town's trade council. It is also easy to exaggerate the success of full-time hairdressers. Some were only nominally full-time: a boy lodging with a Liverpool barber during the early years of the present century remembers that 'There was always great consternation whenever anyone took the barber pole seriously.'[43]

Some working men did make a successful transition to full-time employment in the trade. David Jenkins was one: he had worked underground in the expanding Aberdare Valley coal industry before becoming a hairdresser in 1890 when he was about thirty. Twenty years later he was soundly established in the hairdressing world and a well known figure in local Labour party circles.[44]

Even those who worked assiduously at their calling faced severe and increasing difficulties. The more general use of the safety razor meant that more and more people began to shave themselves. Then, as in so many branches of penny capitalism, ease of entry exacerbated the problems. But the small barber had to face competition not only from other penny shavers, but also from the increasingly threatened established trade. Early in 1910 the hairdressers of Hull circulated the following handbill:

> IF ANY MAN is too mean to pay 1½*d*. for a Good, clean, honest, sanitary Shave, he WANTS TO GROW WARTS on his neck instead, and use them for collar studs; it will save him money; you CAN'T get good studs for less than 12 a penny — MEN — haven't you more respect for your faces than to go to a 1*d*. 'SCAB' SHOP?[45]

To counteract such competition, the small barber always tended to work very long hours. As that voice of the established trade, the *Hairdresser's Weekly Journal*, complained in 1882, 'to pay his small rent and get a bare existence he is obliged to work from dawn til ten, eleven, and even twelve o'clock at night in the chance of picking up some straggler who could not find it "convenient" to leave his public-house companions before'.[46] By the end of the period such rhetoric was being translated into action; in Burton-on-Trent, for example, the local branch of the National Federation of Hairdressers was laying complaints about late opening before the Shop Hours Act Inspector.[47]

There were other, less tangible difficulties. The working-class barber's close identification with his customers — the very foundation of his business — also presented commercial problems. It was not easy to refuse offers of payment in kind, nor indeed to decline to cut hair free 'when things've been on the rough side'.[48] Nor, the final indignity, did the working-class hairdresser and his family necessarily possess the expertise to realise their assets, such as they were. When Walter Greenwood's father died, 'somebody introduced Mother to a gentleman whose honesty could be vouched for though he, too, hadn't any money. He took over father's business and promised to pay the agreed price by instalments. This arrangement he dishonoured, quietly disposing of everything portable for cash, then disappearing without trace.'[49]

It appears unlikely therefore that many penny capitalist barbers managed to earn more than skilled workmen. Even the penny barbers advertising their businesses for sale in the trade press rarely claimed takings of more than two or three pounds a week. In these circumstances it is not surprising that few penny capitalist hairdressers managed, or probably even wanted, to escape their working-class background. There was constant movement between hairdressing and other working-class occupations. Right at the end of the period a member of the Rhondda Valley Hairdresser's Association applied for a transfer ticket to enable him to join the South Wales Miners' Federation without paying the usual one pound entrance fee. There was constant movement too within the trade. When two master hairdressers were forced to give up their businesses in 1910, they were allowed to register for temporary work with the Manchester, Salford and District Journeymen's Society. As one of the men's representatives told the Glasgow Trades Council in the same year, in the hairdressing trade 'there were only a few weeks between employers and employee. If an employer fell ill he was liable to have to join the ranks of the employees when he recovered, so fickle were the customers.'[50]

There is little reason to suppose that, with the one exception of teaching, the nineteenth and early twentieth centuries saw any significant decline in penny capitalist provision of personal services. On the other hand, there is some evidence that it was becoming increasingly difficult for penny capitalists to withstand the tendency towards overcompetition which was so common in any activity with a very low threshold of entry.

9

Financial Services

Virtually nothing is known about working-class provision of financial services. This is not simply because of the elusiveness of the sources but also because money-lenders, pawnbrokers and savings club organisers do not correspond in any way to the 'heroic' working class about which so many labour historians still wish to write. Yet it was not uncommon for working people, and particularly women, to run Christmas clubs, stocking, crockery and other savings clubs all with a single end in view: to make some extra money by easing their neighbours' immediate financial worries. Here Harry Matthews, a Faversham brick worker, describes the club which he ran at the beginning of the First World War:

> we used to call if halfpenny club, I don't know if ever you've heard of it, I used to have the cards printed, and the first week when we started in January, when they started, that first week was ½d. they used to pay. The next week 1d. The week after 1½d., the week after 2d. Used to go up ½d. every time see, till you got to that 1s. 1d., then it used to come back. Half the card going up till you got to that 1s. 1d., and then when you come back it would drop ½d. off, up to Christmas. I forget, but I think when I used to pay them out Christmas, I used to have up to 200 on the books here. I took pretty well over 200 sometimes, what was paid in the club money. Then when it comes to your out, I think it used to come to something about like 28s. 8d. and I used to take the 8d. and give them the 28s.[1]

Even more common was working-class money-lending. But this is another slippery subject with which to deal: not only are the sources elusive, but it is no easy matter to decide the point at which helping a friend became money-lending proper. The most useful distinction is that between loans made with interest and those made without, and it is the former which are the concern here. Lending to friends, neighbours and relatives on a commercial basis was always widespread. It is clear, for example, that penny capitalists active in other spheres also dabbled in money-lending. An eighteen-year-old costermonger was arrested in 1850 for setting himself up as the secretary of a loan society distinguished chiefly, it seems, by its impressive sounding title. Most, however, lent money simply as an extension of their usual activities as street bookmakers, lodging-house keepers, credit drapers, beer sellers or small shopkeepers.[2] Sometimes a money-lending career began almost by accident: 'Next door neighbour wanted to borrow a pound . . . and somebody next door still 'd say, "Ooh, well ask him" like that. They weren't actually professional, they were semi-professional money-lenders'.[3] More often a conscious decision was made, prompted perhaps by a windfall, by some savings or by the job in which the prospective money-lender found himself. When the Elder-Dempster liner, the *Matadi*, sank off the West Coast of Africa in 1896, the widows and mothers of the crew each received three hundred pounds and in Liverpool 'a shrewd few . . . opened up as money lenders'.[4] Foremen were particularly well placed to enter the trade: their relatively high wages provided the capital, and their position the means to put pressure upon reluctant payers. Thus at the turn of the century James Stringer worked as an inspector for the Salford engineering firm of Mather and Platt: 'he started at work lending a shilling to a halfpenny or a shilling to a penny, and it grew and grew'. Eventually he was called into the manager's office and given the choice between money-lending and his job. He chose money-lending.[5] Naturally it is no easy matter to assess the number of those practising what was so often a part-time and secretive calling. In fact evidence is really only available from late-nineteenth and early-twentieth-century Lancashire. Oral testimony reveals that here at least the small money-lender working part-time from home was very common in the large cities. By 1925 there were 1,380 registered money-lenders in Liverpool and Birkenhead, over eighty per cent of them women: 'All the women, and a certain number of men, carrying on business in small streets from their own houses'.[6]

Most of these back-street money-lenders operated if not secretively, then at least inconspicuously. Custom was generated by word of mouth. One coalman money-lender still had a lot of customers on the outskirts of Manchester in the 1920s. 'You see with him being a coalman everybody could be secretive about it whereas, as far as anybody was concerned they didn't do anything like that, but we always knew that if Mr. Howarth was your Coalman, then you were borrowing.'[7] Thereafter methods varied. Some kept a written record of their loans, others did not; certainly none ever furnished their clients with a copy. Some collected their own repayments; the more successful employed agents to do it for them. Nor is it easy to generalise about the interest rates charged, except to confirm that they were invariably extremely high. The cheapest rate anywhere seems to have been one penny a week for each shilling borrowed (8.5 per cent per week, equivalent to 442 per cent per annum). The rate could climb much, much higher — to twenty or even twenty five per cent per week, the interest charged by Warrington money-lenders in the years immediately before the First World War. Moreover, it was not unknown for the borrower to be forced either to purchase an unwanted item or to face an extra charge when the principal and interest were finally repaid.[8]

Like street bookmakers, penny capitalist money-lenders knew — or at least knew of — their clients. Unlike pawnbrokers, however, they did not ask for any security: they 'relied less upon collateral than upon their reputation for administering physical beatings to recalcitrant debtors'.[9] The first step was usually to refuse defaulters any further assistance; the next was to threaten disclosure to their spouse and/or employer; the final step was to threaten, and then inflict, some kind of physical violence (the more successful hiring the euphemistically named 'collectors' to go round and do a little of threatening').[10] Nor were women money-lenders necessarily reluctant to mete out the punishment themselves. In Liverpool at the turn of the century,

Mrs. Mangan, a hard-working washerwoman, borrowed a pound from Sissy Curlett and found herself, after her husband had deserted her, unable either to meet principal or interest. The fact that her husband had deserted her saved her the beating; but from then on the entire Curlett family wash was sent to her weekly — to pay off the interest. One day, Father Corlett found Mrs. Mangan exhausted by the side of her tub, and when she explained that she would have to continue with this payless task to avoid a beating, the good priest's ire was aroused. It heightened considerably when she explained that this weekly washing had been going on for three months and had no definite time limit. In his spiritual capacity he commanded her to stop the washing.

The following week, when Sissy and her sister called with their basket, Mrs. Mangan, filled with spiritual righteousness, told of Father Corlett's order and her intention of complying with the divine command. The Curlett sisters set upon her and beat her into unconsciousness, after which they broke up all the furniture and prized religious pictures.[11]

It is impossible to penetrate behind the lack of firm evidence and the weight of middle-class disapproval, to form any reliable estimate of the profitability of back-street money-lending. Given the prevailing interest rates, it is surely reasonable to assume that, even with the problem of bad debts, substantial profits were often made.

Working-class attitudes towards penny capitalist money-lenders seem to have been ambiguous. Nor is this surprising. For whereas money-lenders often began by doing favours for friends and acquaintances, their profits soon created tensions which separated them from the surrounding community. They were able to enjoy a higher and more secure standard of living than their neighbours. Ron Barnes' grandfather was a Bethnal Green money-lender. His grandmother used to keep up appearances by dressing better than the neighbours, while his grandfather would shun the public bar in favour of the saloon, where he could drink with local bookmakers and stallholders.[12] As with street bookmakers, there was never any doubt as to the class of these penny capitalist money-lenders. Their lack of respectability let them down. No matter what their earnings, they remained firmly entrenched in the

working class. Even the *Pawnbrokers Gazette* could not re-
sist mocking the descriptions which some female money-
lenders gave of themselves when registering under the 1900
Moneylenders' Act: 'dark and of middle height' wrote one;
a 'marrid whoman' (*sic*) declared another.[13]

The other source of working-class credit was of course the
pawnbroker, 'the poor man's banker'. But like money-lending,
casual pawnbroking can be difficult to identify, for presumably it was not uncommon to lend to family and friends on
the security of some possessions. Pawnbroking proper was
less accessible to penny capitalists than money-lending. For
one thing, much skill and experience were needed to judge
the resale value of each pledge. The most profitable pledges
were those redeemed quickly because the same interest was
paid whether goods were held for a day or for a month. Thus
it was thought best to undervalue children's clothing because
after six months or so they might well be of little further use
to their owners.[14] Another difficulty was that the opening of
a *bona fide*, full-time pawnshop required the possession of a
considerable amount of capital. There was the licence to buy,
storage space to provide, pledges to purchase and probably
some time to wait before these were redeemed. Naturally it
needed good connections and/or exceptionally good fortune
for a working man to raise the necessary money. It could
happen. James Bowes' father worked as a pattern maker in
Manchester and also helped at a pawnshop belonging to a
fellow member of the Independent Congregational Church.
In 1880 he managed to borrow, without any security, the
sum of eight hundred pounds from the local philanthropist
Charles Rowley in order to open his own shop. Even then,
the pawnbroker's worries were only just beginning. The
daughter of another pawnbroker's assistant in Manchester
remembers that when he left to work on his own, her mother
'was very concerned about father starting up in business, and
she said to him once, oh John, you know, if you'd had a
sweet shop we could have seen the money coming back over
the counter, but here it's all going out, and of course it is,
in pawnbroking until they start redeeming, you've just got
to have more than stock, you've got to have some capital
behind you'.[15]

If the established trade was normally beyond their reach, middle-aged working people did manage more often to open small, unlicensed, illegal pawnshops. These were known in Scotland as 'wee pawns' and in England and Wales as 'dolly shops', 'receiving shops' or 'leaving shops' because their proprietors *bought* goods on the understanding that they could resell them after a month if they had not been bought back by their original owner. Because they claimed to buy goods rather than to take in pledges, they were able to secure exemption from police licensing and supervision. It was – and is – difficult to distinguish between dealers who accepted goods as payment and those who accepted goods as security for future payment. As a result, perhaps, these illegal pawnshops were often run in conjunction with some other penny capitalist business such as a chandler's, a rag shop, a marine store or a beershop. Because of their illegality, these small pawnbrokers traded covertly, making it difficult to establish their true numbers. The problem is compounded by the tendency of established brokers to exaggerate the extent of this illegal trade. As early as 1839 the Lord Mayor of London presided at a meeting in the Guild Hall where it was claimed that there were some five hundred unlicensed brokers in the metropolis, concentrated not surprisingly in East End areas such as Shadwell and Limehouse. By the middle of the century illegal pawnshops were said to be common in every large manufacturing town in England and Scotland.[16]

It is from Glasgow that the greatest volume of evidence survives. In 1840 there were said to be between 400 and /00 wee pawns in the city, driving one regular pawnbroker to protest that 'The keepers of many of these places are employed as labourers, &c., through the day, and who, having saved a few pounds, adopt this method of eking out their weekly income.'[17] By 1850 there were alleged to be 450 to one thousand wee pawns (compared to forty licensed businesses) and five years later estimates varied from two to three hundred up to five hundred (compared to fifty regular brokers). Thereafter numbers declined fairly rapidly. The Dolly Shop Act of 1856, which imposed heavy penalties for failing to take out a licence, seems to have been successful in the city. There were a number of prosecutions and fifty or more wee pawnbrokers took out licences. It was said that by 1870 only about fifty unlicensed pawnbrokers survived in Glasgow.[18] Illegal pawnbroking was attacked in other parts of the country too. Some towns and cities passed bye-laws or obtained local acts of Parliament. By 1870, for instance, Leeds corporation required all dolly shops and marine store dealers in the city to take out a five shilling annual licence and to record all their purchases for possible inspection. Indeed it is striking that by the end of the period the mouthpiece of the respectable trade, the *Pawnbrokers' Gazette*, carried far fewer complaints of illegal activity than it had in the middle of the nineteenth century.[19]

The unlicensed trade did not disappear however. Yet both regular pawnbrokers and other middle-class observers consistently affected ignorance of the causes of the popularity of what the *Scottish Times* called this 'disreputable description of usury'.[20] The interest rates charged by dolly shops were far higher than the thirty per cent a year which the licensed trade was permitted to ask. In 1850, for example, a sailor from H.M.S. *Victory* received three shillings in a Portsmouth dolly shop for a shawl on the understanding that to buy it back would cost him four shillings. Indeed it was maintained that dolly shops throughout the Whitechapel district of London were making a similar charge of threepence in the shilling, no matter how brief the period of the loan. Not only did dolly shops charge exorbitant rates of interest; they also adopted the very worst habits of the trade. They refused to give tickets or to split pledges; they sometimes sold pledges before they could be redeemed, or shut up shop and left in a moonlight flit. There were all sorts of ways to cheat the customer. In late nineteenth century Manchester, some 'poor pawnbrokers . . . had a ridge in the counter . . . and they put the money on the ledge, but there was a crack in that counter, the woman gets out and she doesn't for shame to come back because she's a penny short, a thousand to one she never reckoned the money up'.[21]

How then did the dolly shop owner manage to maintain his trade? The explanation is simple: for despite the complaints of the respectable, these unlicensed pawnbrokers were essentially complementary to, rather than competitive with, the licensed trade. Unlicensed brokers moved quickly into the growing suburbs which the regular trade was slow to enter. They did their best business late in the evenings and on Sundays – the very time that licensed pawnbrokers were compelled by law to close. They accepted both stolen property and tiny, brittle, bulky or perishable items which it was not worth the while of the established trade, with its fixed interest rates, to consider receiving. In short, the unlicensed pawnbroker filled the gaps left by the licensed trade.[22]

As might be expected, it is virtually impossible to assess the profits of these unlicensed, penny capitalist pawnbrokers. They faced many difficulties. Surprisingly enough even professional informers found it worth their while to harass dolly shop proprietors. As well, some customers pledged goods beyond their value, a practice known as 'duffing'. Others tried to pledge goods which did not belong to them. Husband and wife teams sometimes worked together: on at least one occasion in mid-century Liverpool a woman pledged an item 'belonging' to her husband and the pawnbroker was subsequently compelled to return it to the husband without compensation. Moreover at times of public tension and disorder, such as the Chartist riots at Hanley in the summer of 1842, unpopular pawnbrokers might feel it prudent to return goods to their owners without asking for payment.[23]

Trade varied according to local economic circumstances. Pledging always tended to increase in the autumn as the cold weather drew in. At least in late-nineteenth-century Manchester, many pledges were redeemed before Christmas in order to impress visiting relatives – only for them to be pledged again in the new year. There were other profitable occasions. Some observers believed that the desire of working people to attend the Great Exhibition of 1851 led to a great expansion of trade. Thus it was claimed that before the departure of one excursion train to the Exhibition from Leeds, a single pawnbroker 'received on deposit no less than a bushel and a half of watches'.[24]

Completely contradictory claims were made about the profitability of unlicensed pawnbroking. Some believed that profits were modest, arguing for example that the proprietors of Glasgow's wee pawns were making no more than two pounds a week each in the middle of the century. Others believed that profits were far, far higher. One Glasgow broker claimed to know of concerns with capital assets of £1,500 while another asserted that some wee pawns produced a larger return of capital in one year than regular pawnbrokers could in five. A witness before the 1870 Select Committee on Pawnbrokers cited the case of a wee pawn in Edinburgh in which old clothes dealers were reputed to be spending three hundred pounds a week.[25]

Whatever the truth of the matter, and whatever the ambiguities surrounding the class identity of respectable pawnbrokers, there was not the slightest doubt about unlicensed brokers. They remained firmly of, and in, the working class. If anything, this working-class identity was strengthened as the respectable end of the trade tried increasingly to disassociate themselves from their 'Fagin' image and so upgrade their own social status. But pawnbrokers of all types could at least join with their Birmingham colleague who found himself prevented by the poverty of his customers from branching out further into the retail trade: he consoled himself with the thought that as a pawnbroker, 'You make money while you sleep'.[26]

10

Retailing

Retailing long remained a most popular form of penny capitalist activity. At one time or another almost every working man and woman in the country must have tried to sell something at a profit. A Lancaster man recalls his first incursion into dealing:

> The first deal I ever had I bought a watch for ten shillings
> ... and next day when I was at work on my bench, the
> bosses (*sic*) son was working on the next bench to me. He
> said, 'What's tha' got there Tom?' I said, 'A watch.' He
> said, 'Do you want to sell it?' and I said, 'Yes.' He says,
> 'How much?' I said 'A pound,' and he gave me a pound.
> That was the first deal I ever had. My mother used to say
> our Tom will be a ruckster when he grows up ... and a
> ruckster then was a man who buys and sells ...[1]

Women were even more interested in buying and selling although their efforts were not always appreciated. The wife of one Newcastle railway worker

> was ambitious of making money by the mysterious process
> of 'buying and selling', and to that end attended auction
> sales, bought bargains and advertised them for sale again in
> the local paper. Her triumphs were nothing to father,
> though; he thought the whole thing dishonest, and a reflection on his own ability to earn much money. Moreover, he
> didn't like her gadding about and he had the general fear
> of the railwaymen of that period that their absences would
> be taken advantage of and adultery go on behind their
> backs.[2]

Street trading was also common. Indeed although it is now

widely acknowledged that retailing, like other sectors of the economy, underwent great changes during the course of industrialisation, it is not always realised that street selling, which had been for so long an integral part of the distribution system, continued to offer working men and women the opportunity of starting a modest business on their own account.[3] The great attraction of street selling was of course that it needed neither specialised skill nor large amounts of capital, particularly if undertaken on a part-time basis. The hawker's licence could be overlooked, a barrow could be hired and even a home-made tray or basket would suffice to carry the stock. The stock itself could sometimes be obtained for nothing. Women and children living near the coast or in the countryside seem to have been specially adept at this. Fish were caught, game was poached, corn was gleaned, wild flowers gathered and holly, ivy and misletoe collected for the Christmas trade. A boy brought up in a south Yorkshire village remembers that he and his sister 'were surprised to find so many willing to give a penny for a bunch of wild flowers'.[4] Some husbands too were able to make a contribution: just before the First World War an Oxfordshire agricultural labourer 'earned himself a whole pair of shoes, at 7s. 11d., by mole-catching. He gets a penny each for the moles caught, and then skins them and sells the furs for a penny each.'[5]

It was more difficult for those in the towns, without such opportunities and skills. Samuel Fielden recalls that as a boy in mid-nineteenth-century Todmorden he was sent out to collect sand from the refuse tips at local quarries, 'picking ... the whitest scraps, then taking them home, and with a large white stone beating them up into fine sand'. The sand was then hawked from door to door and sold for a halfpenny a quart 'to the poor people to sprinkle upon their stone-flag floors'.[6] Full-time salesmen went to even greater lengths to obtain stock for nothing. John Babbington recalled that when he met a fellow London hawker in Birmingham around the middle of the century,

> I noticed that he had nearly a whole brick inside his coat and asked what he was going to do with it he laughingly exclaimed well as I just told you this horrible summer has served me as it has you broke my back and this ... brick

is my stock to start me afresh tomorrow I'm going to take it to my lodging grind it into a fine powder then get some clean white paper make it into packets and sell it as a certain remedy against fleas black betles. (*sic*)[7]

More usually in urban areas the hawker had to buy his stock from a shop, a pawnbroker, a market or from a wholesaler — often on a day to day basis. Quacks obtained their medicines from local druggists while every large fruit and vegetable market proved a popular hunting ground for produce which had 'been left over from day to day, and become detiorated in value'. For 'By the side of the wealthy salesmen and wholesale purveyors of fruit, green stuff, and flowers, there are innumerable hangers-on, parasites of the flower world, who seek to pick up the few crumbs that must incidentally fall from the loaded boards and counters where so much is bought and sold.'[8] The hawker unable to afford even a day's stock might still be able to obtain a small loan or make a special bargain with his supplier.[9]

However the stock and equipment was acquired, it was unlikely to have cost a great deal of money. When a Staffordshire pedlar, Thomas Hopkins, was robbed in the summer of 1850, he claimed that the most valuable items stolen from his bundle were a handkerchief, a black cloth and a cashmere shawl. Ten years later Mayhew calculated that even in London it cost no more than 12s. 11d. to start in the ham-sandwich street trade: '2s. for a basket, 2s. for kettle to boil ham in, 6d. for knife and fork, 2d. for mustard-pot and spoon, 7d. for ½ cwt. of coals, 5s. for ham, 1s. 3d. for bread, 4d. for mustard, 9d. for basket, cloth and apron, 4d. for over-sleeves.'[10] Finally, in 1885 an Islington costermonger, Charles Redrupp, was robbed of his cart, a board, a pair of scales and four sacks of potatoes worth in all, he claimed, just £2 14s. 6d. This low capital outlay is vital to any understanding of working-class involvement in the street trades. It explains the continuing popularity of this form of selling and, as will be seen later, helps to account for the low and irregular profits which were made.[11]

This low cost made street selling attractive to the ambitious and destitute alike. Sometimes, no doubt, it was but the cover for begging, prostitution, receiving and other petty crime. The ability to attract a crowd enabled pickpockets to practise their skills while selling from door to door made it easy to 'case' a large number of houses. Sometimes, too, it provided a possible escape route for the ambitious working man. William Davies wanted to be a writer. So as a young man in the 1890s, he 'applied at the local police station for a pedlar's certificate, intending to stock myself with laces, pins, needles and buttons with which I could hawk the country from one end to the other. I . . . would, no doubt, save between nine and ten shillings a week as a hawker.'[12]

More often, the decision to sell was born of poverty and misfortune: it was the last desperate ploy of immigrants, the unskilled, the unemployed, the old, the sick, the victimised and the injured. Indeed setting the destitute to hawking constituted almost a traditional form of welfare provision. Thus in the early years of the nineteenth century the Old Poor Law authorities in Aberdare dealt with at least one applicant for relief by making him a grant of two pounds to enable him to set up in business as a hawker. Charitable organisations continued to deal with the 'deserving' poor in this way. Towards the end of the period John Babbington obtained two pounds towards the purchase of stock from the Charity Organisation Society, while the Manchester Benevolence Society was prepared to make grants of up to twenty pounds to enable the poor to purchase a horse and cart and begin selling. Working people themselves maintained the tradition. As late as 1890 the men employed at the Bestwood colliery in Nottinghamshire decided to subscribe a shilling each to buy a horse and cart for an injured colleague so that he too could earn his living as a hawker. Back in London in 1902, the *Cab Trade Record* drew the attention of its readers 'to the fact that our brother unionist, W. Houghton, still stands on Northumberland Avenue for the purpose of supplying many little articles of use to cabmen, and we would ask any of our members when passing to give him a turn, as he, being a cripple, depends entirely on cabmen for his living'.[13]

The street trades also provided a haven for the seasonally unemployed. In the winter labourers all over the country joined the ranks of the hawkers: 'the Irish, as labourers, can seldom obtain work all the year through, and thus the ranks of the Irish street-sellers are recruited every winter by the slackness of certain periodic trades in which they are largely employed — such as hodmen, dock-work, excavating, and the like. They are, therefore, driven by want of employment to the winter sale of oranges and nuts.'[14] Economic depression and industrial disputes were also 'very prolific sources of itinerancy'. In the mid-nineteenth-century cotton industry,

> many of the hands finding it hard for so many to live in one district without working, disperse themselves over the rural counties, and, partly by begging, and partly by a little dealing at first, just manage to eke out a living, but as they proceed, becoming more practised in the business, and mixing with itinerant dealers and 'dodgers' of all sorts, they gradually become absorbed into some of those deceptive practises (*sic*) by which so many travellers live, and finding they have more liberty, and, at least, as good living, they eventually become so enamoured of a wandering, loose life, that they never return to the family.[15]

Not only did street selling help the enterprising and the destitute; it also performed a real and much needed retailing function among the rapidly growing urban population. Street selling flourished in the nooks and crannies left by the shopkeepers and remained an efficient means both of clearing supplies of fresh food from the markets and of breaking bulk into the tiny units which were all that many of the poor could afford. Indeed even towards the end of the century when there was a choice between different types of retail outlet, many working people still preferred to patronise the familiar and convenient working-class hawker. 'They can't be persuaded that they can buy as cheap at the shops; and besides they are apt to think shopkeepers are rich and street-sellers poor, and that they may as well encourage the poor.'[16]

Nonetheless, it is generally assumed that self-employed street salesmen, like other penny capitalists, were severely squeezed by the centripetal forces of urbanisation and industrialisation. According to David Alexander, 'Itinerant services were a stop-gap between the development of housing suburbs and a comparable development of suburban shops and a transport system which could get the consumer into the central area rapidly at low cost.' He concludes that 'while country peddling was probably in decline the number of people involved in itinerant trading was rising, *at least between the 1830s and 1850s*' (my italics). The impression is left that street selling fell into decline some time during the second half of the century.[17]

Unfortunately it is impossible to calculate precisely the number of self-employed men, women and children who worked full or part-time in the various street trades. The licensing authorities were by-passed and it has already been seen that the census returns always tended to underestimate the prevalence of transitory occupations such as hawking, in which numbers fluctuated during the course of the week, from season to season and according to the prevailing economic situation. Nonetheless, as Alexander himself has suggested, the census returns can be used to provide a rough indicator of the size of the permanent core of full-time street salesmen in England and Wales. Used in this way, the census returns are most suggestive, for they reveal an increase, rather than a decrease, in numbers between 1851 and 1911. Absolute numbers rose two and a half times, from 25,747 in 1851 to 69,347 in 1911. More surprising still, the returns also show an increase in the number of street salesmen compared to the rest of the population: in 1851 there was one such trader to 696 other people; in 1911 one to 520, a relative increase of twenty five per cent. For all their limitations, then, the census figures provide no indication at all of a decline in the permanent core of full-time street sellers.[18]

It is more difficult to estimate the number of casual and part-time salesmen and thus the size of the entire workforce. Mayhew believed, for example, that the 1851 census overlooked more than 40,000 of the 45,000 itinerants at work on the streets of London, an estimate which serves as a timely warning against any complacency in assessing the total size of the workforce during the second half of the century. What seems to have happened, however, is that the country trade was in decline by about 1850. It has been found in the Calder Valley for example that the 1830s and 1840s witnessed a sharp drop in the level of itinerant selling. Even in the most remote areas the spread of shop retailing and the coming of the railways were tending to push the rural street trader into an increasingly marginal role as the seller of novelties at seasonal markets and fairs. But it is important not to exaggerate the decline of the country trade. It remained important in sparsely populated districts like rural Northumberland, while even in counties like Warwickshire villagers at the beginning of this century were still receiving visits from drapers, gypsies selling pegs, pedlars with trays of cotton and, on Fridays, hawkers selling fish.[19] The stagnation of the rural trade was more than counterbalanced by the expansion of selling opportunities in the towns. All the available late-nineteenth and early-twentieth-century oral and autobiographical evidence attests to the fact that street selling, both full-time and part-time, remained of considerable significance and, it would seem, just as common as the census figures would lead one to suppose. Thus when Robert Roberts recalled the area of Salford in which he was brought up at the beginning of this century, he remembered vividly that 'Pedlars without licence, like the hawker with his hand-cart, ... haunted the ways, a permanent part of the common scene'.[20]

It appears therefore that, contrary to the accepted view, there was no numerical decline in street trading during the second half of the nineteenth century. On the contrary, what evidence there is points rather to its continuing growth. The permanent core of full-time traders increased both absolutely and relatively; part-time selling remained very widespread and, if one accepts the not unreasonable assumption that part-time selling probably moved broadly in line with the full-time trade, then the numbers engaged in the entire trade must have moved firmly upwards. Even if this assumption is not accepted, there is still no reason to believe that street selling as a whole went into decline until well after the First World War.

Aside from its resilience, the most striking characteristic of this form of retailing was probably its diversity. Street sellers were as heterogeneous as could be. They ranged from the very young to the very old; from the wretchedly poor to the comfortably off; from Wiltshire 'capitalists with a horse and cart, or wagon, to old women who walk to Frome with a basket and hawk the produce from door to door';[21] from metropolitan 'costermonger capitalists' renting out stock and equipment, to the poor Irish woman whose last desperate resort was 'to sell for a ha'pinny the three apples which cost a farruthing'. Thus rather than try to examine the whole range of itinerant trades, attention will be directed towards two of the most common: the costermonger and the seller of small manufactured goods. Both embraced a wide range of activities.

Under the term 'costermonger' is here included only such 'street-sellers' as deal in fish, fruit, and vegetables, purchasing their goods at the wholesale 'green' and fish markets. Of these some carry on their business at the same stationary stall or 'standing' in the street, while others go on 'rounds'. The itinerant costermongers, as contradistinguished from the stationary street-fishmongers and greengrocers, have in many instances regular rounds, which they go daily, and which extend from two to ten miles. The longest are those which embrace a suburban part; the shortest are through streets thickly peopled by the poor, where duly to 'work' a single street consumes, in some instances, an hour. Men 'working' these carry their wares to any part in which they hope to find customers. The costermongers, moreover, diversify their labours by occasionally going on a country round, travelling on these excursions, in all directions, from thirty to ninety and even a hundred miles from the metropolis. Some, again, confine their callings chiefly to the neighbouring races and fairs.

Thus while there were a good number both of men on 'rounds' and of 'stationary' costermongers who set up their stalls in the street, they were always 'to be seen in the greatest numbers at the London street markets on a Saturday night':

there, and in the shops immediately adjoining, the working-classes generally purchase their Sunday's dinner; and after pay-time on Saturday night, or early on Sunday morning, the crowd . . . is almost impassable. Indeed, the scene in these parts has more of the character of a fair than a market. There are hundreds of stalls, and every stall has its one or two lights . . . One man shows off his yellow haddock with a candle stuck in a bundle of firewood ... whilst the boy shouting 'Eight a penny, stunning pears!' has rolled his dip in a thick coat of brown paper, that flares away with the candle ... and the girl with her basket of walnuts lifts her brown-stained fingers to her mouth, as she screams, 'Fine warnuts! sixteen a penny, fine war-r-nuts'.[22]

While some costermongers specialised in fruit or vegetables or fish throughout the year, most were prepared to deal in whatever produce was most readily available and seemed likely to produce the best profit. Whatever the stock, and however cheaply it had been obtained, it was far too valuable to be discarded simply because it was going bad. Even sympathetic observers reacted with distaste to the methods 'the men adopt to brighten up the remains of yesterday's stock before starting out on a new round, a sight to be borne with perfect equanimity only by one whose wants are supplied through some other channel of trade'.[23] There were all sorts of ways to improve appearances. 'I've boiled lots of oranges,' admitted one London costermonger, 'and sold them to Irish hawkers, as wasn't wide awake, for stunning big uns. The boiling swells the oranges and so makes 'em look finer ones, but it spoils them, for it takes out the juice. People can't find that out though until it's too late.'[24] In mid-century Lancashire hawkers

> purchase, for a very small sum, of the dry fruit dealers, their bad cocoa nuts, the liquid of which has dried up, and the nut becomes altogether bad and light; but to make them heavy and appear good, the ingenious vendor bores a hole in one end, puts in a quantity of water, and stops the hole up with a piece of cork, and blackens it. The water, besides giving weight to the nut, makes it appear fresh and of good quality, taking the place of the milk, by which the quality is judged. They are then taken amongst the factory lads on a Saturday night, and sold for just what they will fetch. When these nuts are broken, they smell very badly and are quite unfit to be eaten.

Nor was it difficult to doctor poor quality fish.

> Different sorts of fish are purchased in the market when

they become stale, and hawked, principally, in the poorest districts and suburbs. Most housekeepers judge the freshness of fish, by the rich or bloody appearance of, and under, the gills, and this is really an excellent test, providing the fish have not been tampered with; but the vendor − knowing well how the article is usually judged − either obtains blood from a slaughter-house, or some place, or calls at a druggist's shop and purchases some vermilion, and rubs it in and about the gills, and so gives it the appearance it would have if it were fresh. A druggist at the northeast part of Manchester, informed me that he had sold hundreds of halfpenny-worths and penny-worths of colouring matter for this purpose, and there could be no mistake about what it was for, as it was generally used in his shop, before his eyes.

There was an almost overwhelming temptation for the petty hawker, with his scanty resources and uncertain future, to try to increase his profitability by using faulty weights and measures. Of all the costermongers, nut-sellers were said to be the most adept at giving short measure:

they sell, generally, by measure, sometimes by weight, but not often; but whether they are sold by weight or measure, the purchaser never gets what the seller professes; their pints are very little more than half-pints, their pounds very little more than half pounds. Some use false scales and weights, and others true ones; but it does not follow that the purchaser gets the proper quantity from the latter, on the contrary, those who keep just weights and measures are always the cleverest hands at 'slumming' (this term is applied to cheating in quantity, by either weight or measure). I have known some of the sharpest give only as many nuts as would lay on the bottom of the measure when turned uppermost! But this can only be done when the purchaser requests the seller to put them into his coat pocket. The cleverest at 'slumming', however, have a way of cheating, which is seldom discovered at the time it is done; it is managed by thrusting the measure into the heap of nuts with one hand, and pretending to heap them on to the top of it with the other; the measure, however, remains empty, or nearly so, and all the buyer gets are those only which he had seen heaped on top of it. This way of measuring is so dexterously performed, that few detect it; some certainly return and complain that they have not got their proper quantity, but never get any more, being told that they were measured before their eyes, and 'examine the measures, are they not proper ones?'[25]

Despite such deceits, costermongers generally charged low prices (or engaged in barter) and sometimes enjoyed a reputation for good quality. As a result the costermonger selling fruit, fish and vegetables from a barrow in the street or market retained a key position in urban food distribution throughout the whole of the nineteenth century. Thus as late as the 1880s Charles Booth found that in south London 'The daily wants of the district are to a great extent supplied by an army of costermongers, who perambulate the streets or take their stands in the market streets or at favourite corners.'[26]

Sellers of small manufactured goods were just as heterogeneous as the costermongers. They ranged all the way from Irish labourers in London who took 'to it in the winter-time when they can get no work';[27] to tallymen in Middlesborough who came 'round to the doors of the workmen's houses offering all kinds of wares on the hire system: a mangle, a thimble, a cupboard, a piano, a gramophone';[28] right up to the 'princes' of the itinerant trade, the thousand or so 'Cheap Johns' who travelled with their families to fairs, markets and towns all over the country selling cutlery, firearms, saddlery and other sorts of manufactured products. The trade as a whole included

> many of the very old and the very young; the diseased, crippled, maimed and blind . . . The rest of the class may be described as merely street-sellers; toiling, struggling, plodding, itinerant tradesmen . . . The street-trade in metal manufactured articles is principally itinerant. Perhaps during the week upwards of three-fourths of those carrying it on are itinerant, while on a Saturday night, perhaps, all are stationary, and almost always in the street-markets.[29]

At Petticoat Lane, for instance, 'Those who have something showy, noisily push their trade, while the modest merit of the utterly cheap makes its silent appeal from the lower stalls, on which are to be found a heterogeneous collection of such things as . . . damaged lamps, chipped china shepherdesses, rusty locks and rubbish indescribable.'[30]

Like the costermonger, the typical petty hawker of manufactured goods was prepared to deal in anything small which he could obtain and which he thought he would be able to resell at a profit. There were many like the rag-and-bone man who went round the Cornish villages 'with his little spring balance and an unfailing supply of pennies hidden somewhere on his person'.[31] Every branch of the manufactured trade had its own patter and selling techniques. Watchsellers, for example, worked the streets in the summer but moved indoors to pubs and beershops during the winter while, to evade the auction licence, 'Cheap Johns' often resorted to mock 'Dutch auctions' in which goods were knocked down from a high starting price. Needles were cheap, small and easily broken down into small lots. In Lancashire, for example,

> Fellows dressed as distressed workmen, generally they have a white apron twisted round their bodies, and a paper cap on their heads, arrest the attention of people in the streets, in the same manner as nearly all the street-dealing imposters do, namely, by 'pattering'. The needle dodger, having selected a street corner, in a good thoroughfare, opens his box, if he has one, or spreads his pocket handkerchief, or a sheet of brown paper, on the pavement, and, having arranged his needles thereon, immediately commences the 'patter', which is in these words:—
> 'My friends! I am a needle maker from Redditch, in Worcestershire, where I worked for many years for Mister Blank, who is now stopt for want of work. Kind friends, so bad is our trade now, that I've been out of employ for six months, and I've a wife and three children to support, and, kind friends, they cannot live upon nothink. So, kind friends, I've made a few needles of the very best sort, which I'm selling at a penny a packet; the same needles, kind friends, as is sold in the shops at twopence-ha'penny a packet; but, my friends, people cannot starve. So you see, my friends, what our trade has come to!'[32]

Thus it was by a combination of buying and selling cheaply, adopting a variety of selling techniques and cheating the customer that costermongers and hardware men — like all street traders — were able to earn their living. Yet only rarely was it an easy or comfortable living. This is not to deny of course that even the least successful hawker could occasionally hope to make good money. 'Holidays and idle days are golden days', it was said, 'to nearly all who earn their bread in open spaces, thoroughfares, or streets.'[33] One morning towards the middle of the century John Babbington spent 7½d. on ten cups and saucers from a Birmingham swag shop. He went to the city fair, sold his stock and used the money to buy more; by the end of the day, when he had been able to do this several times, he found that he had accumulated 6s. 9d. a thousand per cent profit on the day's trading. A handful of traders managed to achieve permanent economic security. Michael Marks came to Leeds as a refugee from Poland, began peddling in the surrounding farming and mining villages, opened a stall in Leeds market, expanded into other local towns and went on to found that High Street institution, Marks and Spencer. More modestly, according to Booth, London costermongers 'of the upper grade are a very well-to-do set; they have a valuable property in their stock, &c.; they sometimes have both stall and barrow, working as a family; and some step up into the shop keeping class by establishing the wife in a small shop, while the man still goes round with the barrow'.[34]

These, however, were the exceptions which proved the rule. For if the low capital cost of starting to sell in the streets did much to ensure the continuing popularity of this branch of retailing, it also encouraged fierce competition and contributed to the low and fluctuating profits which were all that most hawkers could ever hope to make. The great majority of street traders lived in chronic insecurity, with inexperience, illness, bad weather and bad luck all posing a constant threat to their livelihood. It was never easy to break into the trade successfully. Newcomers were specially likely to be sold short measure by the wholesalers and always, it seems, found it difficult to push themselves forward. Thus during the Lancashire cotton famine some workers, in

desperation, began to sell newspapers, religious tracts and
back numbers of penny periodicals but it was 'easy to see,
from their shy and awkward manner, that they are new to
the trade, and do not like it'.[35] A similar situation occurred
towards the end of the century when Roland Kenny rented a
stall in Accrington market. 'I shouted Mollie's wares and tried
to shepherd reluctant housewives to the stall. It reminded me
somewhat of my newsboy days, when I yelled '*Manchester
Mail* or *News*; *Oldham Chron-icle* or *Stan-daard*' in the streets
of Leeds and Springhead. I have no idea what I shouted on
Accrington market ground. At my first attempt I became
horribly self-conscious, and all I emitted was a croak . . .'[36]

Once started in business, there were continual difficulties.
There was danger from the traffic and from bored or light-
fingered passers-by. There was police harassment, competition from the growing number of general shops, and complaints of obstruction from local residents, shopkeepers,
credit drapers, commercial salesmen and other 'respectable'
hawkers. A Wolverhampton man complained in 1850 that his
'town has been inundated for the last five days by a set of
people who get their living by attending fairs, and our streets
. . . have been blocked up by booths and shows, making it a
difficult matter for the respectable shopkeepers to leave their
houses, or for any lady to get into their shops . . . there is
no necessity now for fairs, with our weekly markets, capital
shops, and railway connection'.[37] Later in the century there
were also new local bye-laws to contend with. In 1883, for
instance, Yarmouth corporation framed a code of bye-laws
including one forbidding the carriage of goods for sale
between seven o'clock in the evening and five o'clock in
the morning.[38]

As if all this was not enough, demand could be affected by
factors utterly outside the hawker's control. A London costermonger remembered an outbreak of cholera when 'people
became so frightened at the very name of fruit that my trade
was almost at an end'.[39] The weather was perhaps the greatest
worry of all. In Glasgow the poor Spring of 1895 'put a stop
to a great deal of work . . . those doing little peddling trades
could not go out, and got behindhand'.[40] In London too,
the flower girls were 'greatly dependent on the weather, for

it not only influences the price of flowers, but the wet reduces the number of loiterers who are their best customers'.[41] In fact, one clergyman assured Mayhew, 'Three wet days will bring the greater part of 30,000 street-people to the brink of starvation.'[42] Certainly adverse weather soon dashed the high hopes of William Davies who, it was seen earlier, started out confident of earning enough money to set himself up as a writer.

> I reached Northampton, and it was in this town that I intended to start business on the following day, though I still had a few shillings left, having slept in the open air since leaving London. With this object I proceeded to examine my pack, with the intention of filling my pockets with the different wares, to draw them forth one or two at a time, as they would be needed. So, that night, previous to the great business that was to be transacted on the following day, I sought a quiet corner in the lodging house, and began to unroll my paper parcel. As I proceeded to do this, it seemed to me that the inner part of the parcel was damp, and then I remembered the two or three heavy showers that we had on the second day of my travels. On a further examination I discovered, to my horror, that the goods were entirely unfit for sale: that the parcel had been so bent and misshapen one way and the other, during my night's repose, that the needles had cut through their rotten packets, and were stuck in the pin papers, and that a great number of pins had concealed their whole bodies in the needle packets, showing plainly the guilty tops of their heads. The laces were twisted and turned, and their tags were already rusted.[43]

The result of all this was that profits fluctuated alarmingly. They varied sharply from day to day: a mid-century London dealer spent 35s. on 'snuffers, knives and forks, iron candlesticks, padlocks and bed-screws' and during the following week his profits ranged from three shillings on Monday, to 2s. 3d. on Tuesday, 1s. 6d. on Wednesday, nothing at all on Thursday, 3s. on Friday, and 6s. 1d. on Saturday morning and evening, a return of forty five per cent on his week's trading. During the whole of the subsequent week he was able to make only 1*s*. 5¼*d*. – a stark reminder indeed of the trade's constant uncertainty. Profits also fluctuated seasonally. Mayhew was the best informed of all contemporary commentators and he reported that in mid-century London, costermongers' profits varied from perhaps 30*s*. a week during the summer fruit season to as low as four shillings a week in the winter when 'the street-sellers of fruit and vegetables are cut off from the ordinary means of gaining their livelihood . . . These calculations give an average of about 14*s*. 6*d*. a week, when [and if] a man pursues his trade regularly.'[44] It was the same in the metropolitan flower trade. The girls' income varied 'considerably according to the season. In the summer months, more than a pound net profits have been cleared in a week; but in bad weather these women have often returned home with less than a shilling as the result of twelve hours exposure to the rain.'[45]

There is not the slightest doubt that selling in the streets was a precarious, and often unpleasant, way of earning a living. Booth found, for example, that in the east end of London in the 1880s, the number of street traders living below the poverty line outnumbered those above it by at least two to one. But this must not be allowed to obscure the importance of the outdoor trades to working-class life throughout the period. Mayhew put it succinctly: 'the class of travelling tradesmen are important, not only for forming a large portion of the poor themselves, but as being the persons through whom the working people obtain a considerable part of their provisions and raiment.'[46]

Street traders were unambiguously working class. Provincial hawkers banded together to deal with local market companies while London costermongers formed trade unions which organised benefit concerts, were active in local conservative politics, and even put forward their own parliamentary candidates. Even those with social aspirations could not deceive their neighbours. Underneath Arthur Harding there

lived a family named Ward that had a fish stall in Brick Lane market. A man and a woman. They sold kippers and bloaters and they used to keep them under the bed. The smell was continuous so you very rarely noticed it. They only had one room and all they had on that stall went into the room because you couldn't trust it out in the yard – the people would be knocking it off. They only had a barrow – a barrow and a board – but Mr Ward fancied himself, and thought that being a stall-keeper he was a cut above the layabouts: he reckoned himself a tradesman even though he did it all from a single room.[47]

Hawkers, hucksters, pedlars, duffers, tallymen and coster-mongers all had an unsavoury reputation with working class and middle class alike. Costermongers were particularly un-popular neighbours with London artisans because they mono-polised the water supply in preparing their vegetables. Hawkers too were often regarded with distrust. 'They were like what they call now the "fly-boys",' explains the daughter of a Canterbury coalman, 'You see they knew, if there was some-thing going they went after it. Made their money that way.'[48] Amongst the middle class, street selling was a byword for un-acceptable behaviour. Jack the Ripper's victims, it was noted, included street sellers. Such was the disdain in which the street trades were held that when a meeting of 'The Hair-dressers' Guild' was disrupted in the winter of 1882, it was said that the intruders behaved appallingly, 'in a manner that would disgrace Whitechapel costermongers'.[49]

The same desires and pressures which drove the destitute and casually employed to sell on the streets encouraged their better-off neighbours to open beerhouses and small corner shops. For some, this represented the culmination of years of dreaming and saving. For many more, it offered a traditional refuge from economic adversity. Not surprisingly, the drink trade held many attractions. Widows and industrial accident victims were sometimes helped to open beershops by work-mates or by the parish authorities. Others needed no such en-couragement: during the Lancashire cotton famine, for example, at least one unemployed factory worker tried to sell home-made bitter from his cottage for a halfpenny a bottle. Others went through more formal channels. Within a month of the closure of the Blaina ironworks in South Wales in May 1867, there were seventeen applications for new beershop licences at the local licensing sessions.[50] Other types of shop-keeping were also popular. In fact running a small shop be-came somewhat easier as the spread of factory produced and widely advertised goods reduced the role of the retailer in the preparation and presentation of his stock. Certainly by the end of the century it was not unusual for the unemployed, the victimised, the abandoned, the injured and the bereaved to begin selling from their homes. It was said that corner shops in Bolton were 'small cramped stores usually kept by disabled miners or widows', while in the Fife mining village of Fordell 'The colliery owners . . . allowed a widow to use one room in her house as a "sweetie shop" with a small counter and a window for the display of her goods. Here was sold sweeties, rock, the smallest of the kitchen and household articles, such as a packet of pins, thread, penny bottles of vinegar, penny packets of note paper.'[51]

Thus the capital cost of opening a shop or beerhouse, though higher than that of beginning to hawk, was by no means beyond the reach of many ordinary working-class families. It was not expensive to take down the parlour curtains, make a counter, install a hogshead or fill the window with goods, and open the front door to customers. Parlour publicans and shopkeepers were common everywhere and a South Wales miner remembers that before World War I he 'saw only a very few real shops in the village — most of the selling was done in houses that had converted their front rooms into shops and hung outside signs advertising tea or salmon'. After the War his 'wife caught the craze for shop-keeping, so I had made a counter and shelves, and our front room was a shop'.[52] Even the cost of renting purpose-built premises was not necessarily prohibitive and there was always the possibility of postponing the first two or three weeks' rent until it could be paid for out of the takings. Booth, for example, found a small shopkeeper who paid 3s. 6d. a week for a 'shop' consisting of 'a wooden screen betwixt door and fire, two tables, a counter, small and large scales and weights, a good corner cupboard, and some odds and ends'.[53] Even towards the end of the century fairly substantial premises could still be found reasonably cheaply. One 1883 issue of the *Fish Trades Gazette*, for example, contained details of a fish and chip shop off Kings Cross, London for rent at five shillings a week and of another available in the south-west of the city for 12s. 6d. a week.[54]

In many shops some at least of the stock could be obtained for next to nothing, thus obviating the need to tie up large sums of money. Food shops could be especially cheap to start. The daughter of a dockyard worker from Rochester in Kent remembers that when her father was running his own greengrocery business at the end of the century, he used to breed rabbits in the backyard for sale at Christmas and was quite prepared to walk out to meet the market gardeners on their way into town. 'The further you walked the cheaper you'd buy.'[55] Many women turned their culinary skills to profitable use. The wife of a labourer at the Lune mills in Lancaster was not untypical. According to her daughter, 'She used to make her own meat and potato pie and bʸ then she had a gas stove and do them in there and then a big pan of marrow fat peas cooking so it was pie and peas. On a Friday it used to be pie and fritters and the fritters was dipped in batter, and fried in deep fat. Sliced potatoes dipped in fat and fried. So many for a penny. People used to come to the door for these. The neighbours round about used to come for them.'[56] Stock could be obtained cheaply for other types of shop too. 'Boiled boot' shops still flourished in Middlesborough at the beginning of this century. '"Boiled" boots are old boots begged, found in the street, etc, picked up, patched, polished, and sold at a low price.'[57] At least in the more viable small shops, the stock could probably be bought on credit. Robert Roberts recalls that,

> In the struggle for solvency corner-shop economics demanded a wily system of trading. My mother kept grocery travellers from two different wholesalers on what she gleefully called the 'hop'. Each arrived hopefully on different days and, monthly, a pair of rival patent medicine men called too. By getting goods from all these, then settling with one until the others grew restive, she stretched her credit to the uppermost, a necessity in a shop with so many doubtful 'trust' customers. One of her subterfuges infuriated me. Immediately our grocery traveller had left the shop with his order she would despatch me to the warehouse two miles across the town, whence I would return with 24 lbs of packet tea, or with half a roll of bacon lolling over a weary shoulder, and all my play-time gone.

Since goods ordered from a traveller one day were delivered by cart the next, I was convinced that she devised these trips merely to keep me occupied. She did not stoop to explain her economic stratagems to small boys. Only much later did I discover that any items ordered after the traveller's visit did not appear on the current week's invoice. The trick brought still another few days' vital credit. And how we needed them![58]

The task facing the penny capitalist shopkeeper was essentially the same throughout the whole country over the whole period, whether the 'shop' was run part-time by the wife or organised full-time by the whole family. The task was always to minimise the amount of capital and maximise the amount of labour which needed to be injected into the business.

Whatever the cash-flow difficulties, running a shop seemed to offer advantages that selling in the street never could. If, as has been suggested, 'those with pretensions to social status showed little inclination' for a career in selling,[59] there was no corresponding lack of enthusiasm among working people. A boy brought up in Cumberland in the 1890s remembers that his 'grandmother, like many girls brought up to the hard labour of the land, had a great respect for the retail trade and its ancillaries'.[60] In Salford too, 'The less ambitious among skilled workers had aims that seldom rose above saving enough to buy the ingoing of a beer-house, open a corner shop or get a boarding house at the seaside.'[61] Shopkeeping appeared to promise all that was lacking in other working-class jobs: comfort, security, independence and status. The shop itself played a key role in community life. In one late-nineteenth-century Scottish village, for example, 'The Store took the place of the local newspaper, and when any bit of spicey news or news of any importance came in from the outside, one heard the expression on every side, "I'll need tae gaun tae the Store tae see if it's true".'[62] Even more crucial was the shopkeepers' power to grant or withhold credit. Bill Collier remembers that shopkeepers in the Hankey Park district of Salford were the most important local residents 'because if mother wanted to borrow a shilling or a couple of shillings, you know, I used to go and say "Mother wants to know will you lend her two shillings well father gets paid"'.[63] Meanwhile, in a nearby store,

Robert Roberts' mother was trying to assess the credit-worthiness of her customers.

> A wife (never a husband) would apply humbly for tick on behalf of her family. Then, in our shop, my mother would make an anxious appraisal, economic and social – how many mouths had the woman to feed? Was the husband ailing? Tuberculosis in the house, perhaps. If TB took one it always claimed others; the breadwinner next time, maybe. Did the male partner drink heavily? Was he a bad time keeper at work? Did they patronise the pawnshop? If so, how far were they committed? Were their relations known good payers? And last, had they already 'blued' some other shop in the district, and for how much? After assessment credit would be granted and a credit limit fixed, at not more than five shillings' worth of foodstuffs in any one week, with all 'fancy' provisions such as biscuits and boiled ham proscribed. Or the supplicant might be turned down as 'too risky', after which she would trudge the round of other shops in the neighbourhood while the family waited hungry at home. With some poor folk, to be 'taken on at a tick shop' indicated a solid foot at last in the door of establishment. A tick book, honoured each week, became an emblem of integrity and a bulwark against hard times. The family had arrived.[64]

There can be little doubt that opening a small shop or beerhouse remained the dream of any number of working people. Yet it is as difficult to discover the number of aspiring publicans and shopkeepers who managed to transform their dreams into reality as it was to estimate the number of penny capitalists selling in the streets. Many – perhaps most – working-class-owned shops and beerhouses were run by women on a part-time basis, with the result that they rarely appear in the census returns. All over the country husband and wife teams began to run small beershops after the passing of the 1830 Beer Act. The members of the 1833 Select Committee on the Sale of Beer listened with alarm to reports of beershops being run by working people of all kinds: by labourers in Sussex villages; by foremen and subcontractors in Liverpool; and at Whitchurch in Oxfordshire by 'generally broken-down tradesmen and mechanics, and often people of indifferent character, or people that are too idle to work'.[65] Even worse intelligence was received from some of the larger towns and cities where, it was claimed, beershops were in the hands of the most unsuitable people. At Pilkington in Lancashire, the committee was told, the beershops were run 'principally by the very lowest of people', some of whom had even been on poor relief.[66] Within three years of the passing of the Beer Act every village had its own beerhouse. Many had several and even small towns had scores of them: Boston in Lincolnshire had fifty six or seven, Paulton in Somerset ninety one. In larger towns and cities numbers naturally climbed much higher: Leeds boasted 251 licensed beershops (compared to 280 ale houses), Sheffield had 280 (compared to 386) and Liverpool had between 500 and 600 (as opposed to about 1,200 public houses). Despite the tighter licensing controls introduced in 1872, numbers remained high. Still at the very end of the century, there were fifteen beerhouses (as well as a hotel and two off-licences) to cater for the three thousand people living in Robert Roberts' district of Salford.[67]

Of course not all beerhouse proprietors remembered to take out the necessary licences. No doubt illegal drinking was as old as liquor licensing itself, but by the middle of the century illegal shebeens were concentrated chiefly in the industrial regions. In England these shebeens went under a number of aliases: 'wabble shops' in Wolverhampton, 'flash houses' or 'bush houses' in the Black Country, 'hush shops' in Lancashire, and 'dram shops' in North Staffordshire and the rest of the north of England. Oldham hush shops were particularly notorious: there were said to be 387 of them in 1851, 94 of which were run by widows and 217 by proprietors with at least one other source of income. The pages of the *Licensed Victuallers Gazette* continued to be littered with stories of working people prosecuted for running shebeens. In the first six months of 1873 there were reports from Gas Street, Middlesborough, of Margaret McBride selling spirits in her room; from Great Harwood near Bolton of William Greenwood serving beer to his neighbours from a barrel in the kitchen; and from Liverpool of Elizabeth Morgan being sentenced to fourteen days' hard labour for selling beer to a group of at least

five men and ten women. It is unfortunate that there is no
way of extrapolating from such reports of successful prosecutions the true incidence of illegal, worker-run drinking places
in England as a whole.[68]

It is clear, however, that the Sunday closing legislation
introduced into Scotland and Wales in the early 1850s and
1880s respectively did a great deal to stimulate penny capitalist involvement in unlicensed drinking houses. Again statistical precision is unattainable; but from the (admittedly unreliable) evidence of police prosecutions, it would appear that
the number of Scottish shebeens reached a peak soon after the
imposition of Sunday closing. In Edinburgh for instance
there were 445 convictions between 1855 and 1861, but only
forty six in the year from 1890 to 1896. A similar pattern
emerged in Wales where the Sunday Closing Act of 1881 led,
in Cardiff at least, to the opening of a great number of shebeens, many of them run by most unlikely penny capitalists —
the Irish navvies building the city's Barry docks. The statistics
of police prosecutions support the contemporary view that
within a decade or so the problem had been brought under
some sort of control. The evidence is consistent and shows
that in no part of England, Wales or Scotland was it unknown
for better-off working people to open beershops and for their
less prosperous neighbours to organise shebeens. Indeed the
evidence, for all its weaknesses, does seem to suggest that this
form of penny capitalist activity was growing towards the end
of the century.[69]

Part-time trading was not confined to the sale of intoxicat-
ing liquor. Working-class families also played their part in the
expansion of fixed shop retailing during the second half of
the century although the inherent elusiveness of these tiny,
generally part-time, and often transitory businesses again
makes it hard to establish their numerical importance. It is
clear, however, that they were far more widespread than has
generally been supposed. Charles Booth found, for example,
that during the final years of the century, 2.7 per cent of the
population in the east end of London were dependent for
their living on small shops — most of which, it would appear,
were run by working people of one sort or another. Oral
sources in particular confirm the prevalence of part-time shop-

keeping right to the end of the period. In her pioneering study of the working class in Barrow-in-Furness and Lancaster between 1890 and 1914, Elizabeth Roberts discovered that 'only four of the respondents' mothers out of 75 earned a full second income for the family. There were, however, 24 others employed on a casual part-time basis. Their occupations are not enumerated in the census returns but their financial contributions to their families could be of considerable significance . . . two opened shops in their parlours to sell home-made pies and cakes, four helped their husbands in their small corner shops . . .'[70] The parlour shop and beershop remained the most accessible forms of self-employment available to those seeking independence or extra income but lacking capital and specialised skills.

Running these small businesses was never easy. Every member of the family was expected to help during the long hours that needed to be worked to make any sort of profit. Throughout the century pubs and beershops were allowed to open from six o'clock or earlier in the morning until ten or eleven at night, only closing completely on Sunday mornings. Even these hours were not long enough for some landlords; to extend his trade to Sunday morning, one mid-century Wolverhampton beerhouse owner 'adopted the expedient of making a hole through the wall of his house into the house occupied by his tenant, and in whose house the company sat to drink'.[71] Shop hours were no shorter. It was not until 1918 that Robert Roberts' mother 'happily contrasted the times with those around the turn of the century with its sixteen-hour day (7 a.m. till 11 p.m.), 400 customers a week and a gross weekly taking of about £7'.[72] According to the daughter of another Lancashire parlour shopkeeper, 'I never knew anyone burn so many meals, every day you went in our kitchen we had a pan soaking that was burnt, every day. Because every day she was in the shop and forgot the meal.'[73]

It was in dealing with their customers that working-class shopowners enjoyed their major advantage over their rivals. 'Indeed, a working-class background and consciousness could be a precious asset. Such men knew their future markets instinctively and innately.'[74] Their shops were simple; their customers were drawn from friends and neighbours; the service was unpretentious; and credit was available. 'Open a little house shop and you patronised them and war betide you if they didn't. As far as my mother was concerned and most of them was like my mother, go to Mrs. Dixons or Mrs. Greaves and they used to go round and share out the patronage. My mother would send round to different shops.'[75] Customers expected to be able to continue the earlier street practice of haggling over the price. So even on the eve of the First World War in the Bayswater district of London, meat was 'often bargained for and sold by the piece without weighing. The experienced house-wife offers so much, while the ticket on the meat is offering it for so much more. A compromise is arrived at and the commodity changes hands.'[76] Both shop-keepers and publicans, like street-traders, tried to repair their profit margins by adulterating the stock and using false weights and measures. In Salford Robert Roberts' father's quarter of a pound 'varied from three and a half to five ounces, according to the customer's face, reputation and antecedents.' Yet he bitterly resented the stratagems adopted by other traders. 'A favourite trick of some publicans, well enough known to our imbibers, was to dilute their ale, then add salt to "flavour it up" and stimulate thirst. My father, who loved liquor as he loved life, considered this to be a crime that called for the ultimate penalty.'[77]

Any assessment of the profitability of working-class-owned shops and beerhouses is beset with the same difficulties that plague the study of all forms of penny capitalism. Reliable records were rarely kept: in one late-century Preston parlour shop, for example, 'Everything went in the till and everything came out of the till. There was no such thing as bookkeeping . . . Any income-tax papers were thrown on the fire. We would get jail for it today.'[78] Certainly there were very serious obstacles in the way of economic success. In beerhouses and small shops alike it was difficult to control troublemakers and hard to prevent pilfering. A Rochester (Kent) woman remembers the problems in her father's greengrocers. He used 'to have kids put their hands round the corner of the door and pinch an apple or an orange or something like that' and on one terrible occasion 'I gave half a sovereign away for a farthing, and I was only about seven. I knew who I gave it to, but they didn't, you know.'[79] Patrick McGeown remembers the grocery store which the Murphys ran in Craigneuk, about twelve miles from Glasgow, at the start of this century,

> The Murphy family were the only Irish I knew who had pulled themselves out of the pick and shovel range. Indeed they hadn't travelled far, for the business was teetering on the unsteadfast footing of a spear. I heard my father say so to my mother, only not knowing Shakespeare he put it a different way. For success Mr Murphy needed rid of two things, one was young Paddy who stole half the stock, and the other was Mrs Murphy who gave the other half away. She had a kind heart and as most of the customers had no money and consciences to match, the kind heart ticked while the tick was mounting.[80]

Some shopkeepers responded in kind. The widow of a Manchester warehouseman opened a small shop. But 'Whilst mother was serving people they were lifting things out of the shop that was on show, and ultimately I think she got very much into debt. And like other people of those times she did a moonlight. I think they moved about four or five o'clock in the morning, back to where we'd come from in Higher Crumpsall.'[81]

Moreover the right sort of personality was essential. Publicans and beerhouse proprietors needed to be on their guard against the attractions of their stock. A young man employed in the turning-shop of the Kilmarnock railway works in the 1850s 'was putting on the belt of his lathe, and had his arm torn away from the shoulder'. Although he had not been a member of the Amalgamated Society of Engineers long enough to qualify for their disablement grant, a collection was made and this raised £140. 'He opened a public-house, which in two years wrecked the moral man worse than the shaft did the physical.'[82] The son of a Preston fish and chip shop owner recalls that his father too was unsuited to his job. 'One needed to be able to talk football, horse racing and pass on bets, plus saucy tales to the right people at the right time.'[83] There were other difficulties. To the police and many members of the middle class, the pub was bad, the beershop worse, and the shebeen quite intolerable. An outstanding, though untypical, indication of such attitudes is provided by the 'Huddersfield Crusade' which Superintendent Tom Heaton led against local beerhouses in the middle of the century. To encourage prosecutions he allowed his parish constables a shilling witness fee as well as a percentage of any fine which was imposed upon conviction.[84]

The most serious difficulty confronting the small trader was that of bad debts, a problem aggravated by the ebb and flow of local economic conditions. The son of a working-class Kent shopkeeper put it succinctly: 'if you didn't give any credit you never got any trade'; if you did give credit, you often did not get it back.[85] Even the apparent advantage of having friends and neighbours for customers had its drawbacks. A working-class publican from Kent recalls one of the problems: 'in those little places you see . . . if you offended one, you offended a lot, because they were all relatives more or less you see, so you had to be very careful, who you upset.'[86] Moreover the difficulties under which all small retailers laboured were considerably magnified towards the end of the nineteenth century with the advent of postal selling, co-operative shops and later of national and provincial multiple stores. It has been estimated for example that the proportion of national salary spent in the co-ops increased from 4.2 to 11.4 per cent between 1880 and 1913, and that they took trade particularly from independent butchers, drapers, clothiers, furnishers and grocers. It has been further estimated that by 1900 the co-ops and multiples together accounted for about twenty per cent of the grocery and provision trade, a figure which had risen to about thirty per cent by 1915.[87]

The line between success and failure was a tenuous one. Inexperience, sheer economic incompetence, bad luck, bad weather, economic depression, an unhelpful supplier or an unscrupulous landlord could all drag a family down. When a special correspondent from the *Manchester Examiner and Times* visited 'a poor provision shop' in Preston during the cotton famine, he reported that 'Their's was a family of seven — man, wife and five children. The man was a spinner; and his thrifty wife had managed the little shop, whilst he worked at the mill . . . A few months' want of work, with their little stock of shop stuff oozing away — partly on credit to their poor neighbours and partly to live upon themselves — and they became destitute of all, except a few beggarly remnants of empty shop furniture.'[88]

Disasters of the magnitude of the Lancashire cotton famine were exceptional of course. But all over the country would-be entrepreneurs succumbed, one at a time, to the hard facts of economic life.

> Fiascos were common; again and again one noticed in the district pathetic attempts to set up shops in private houses by people who possessed only a few shillings' capital and no experience. After perhaps only three weeks one saw their hopes collapse, often to the secret satisfaction of certain neighbours who, in the phrase of the time, 'hated to see folk trying to get on' . . . 'CURRAN CAKES 3 for 2*d*.' advertised one neighbour on a little pile of grey lumps in her house window. Nobody bought. We children watched them growing staler each day until the kitchen curtain fell again on the venture like a shroud.[89]

It is not easy to weigh the catastrophes of some against the successes of others. No two outlets did exactly the same business. In the small Wiltshire village of Corsley, for instance, three women kept shops to supplement their families' other earnings. It was found that 'One of them does a good business, but little is done by the others, the people of Corsley now [1909] buying their provisions mainly from the towns, or from people who hawk round from door to door.'[90] As in all forms of penny capitalism the distinction between the part-time business and the more or less full-time was crucial. As a representative of the Manchester Shopkeepers and Small Traders' Protection Association pointed out in 1906, 'I distinguish clearly between those who live in their shops, work them themselves, and whose motives are merely to obtain a living, and those who live away from their busines (*sic*) are compelled to employ assistants, and whose motives over and above a living are increasing profits and dividends.'[91] So long as the business was run on a part-time basis, to provide a second source of income, no great harm would probably be done if the enterprise proved less successful than anticipated. But whenever the business provided a family with its sole, or major, source of income, failure was infinitely more serious. In fact most concerns probably neither succumbed nor succeeded particularly well. Even full-time shops provided their owners with a living little better than those of the working-class families whom they served and among whom they continued to live. But, as Booth remarked, 'It may reasonably be assumed that if they do not drop out of existence as shops, profit is on the whole to be found in the business.'[92]

Of course the success of a beerhouse or parlour shop was not to be measured solely in economic terms. The wife of a Barrow-in-Furness shipwright explained to her daughter that when her husband became unemployed in the 1890s, 'One of the things she started to do, she was a pretty good baker and she would sell some of her bread and gradually this developed into a little parlour shop selling bacon, cheese and all sorts of commodities . . . She told me it wasn't that it made much money this little shop but it made her a help in the house.'[93] Even though part-time shopkeepers did not seek — and full-time shopkeepers rarely managed — to rise economically out of the working class, the latter's desire for independence and upward mobility did tend to set them apart. A girl brought up in a Preston parlour shop remembers that her family enjoyed a higher standard of living than the neighbours but, more importantly, 'We thought we were better than the rest but we didn't show it. Because we worked for it, that was the real reason, we've tried and the effort is there.'[94] The shop met social as well as economic needs; it had an importance over and above the income which it generated. Norman Nicholson's father refused to leave his Cumberland shop to fight in the First World War. 'It was not, however, on his own account that he insisted on staying home. He had a wife, he had a child, he had a shop, and he felt a moral obligation to all three. And not least to the shop. When he said he kept a shop he did not just mean that the shop kept him. He was bound to the shop as he was to his wife and looked on bankruptcy as almost the same as adultery.'[95]

For all their contribution to the expansion of the nineteenth-century distributive system, working-class hawkers, landlords and shopkeepers remain decidedly shadowy figures. Yet penny capitalism performed a vital role in the retail trade, as in so many other facets of nineteenth-century economic and social life. It was possible to enter retailing in so many different ways. It provided a dream, a possible escape route from poverty and drudgery. If hopes of comfort, security and status almost always proved illusory, it was often 'easier for an unskilled worker to attain a crisis-ridden insecurity, but apparent independence, as a small dealer or shopkeeper, than to enter the main crafts'.[96] Penny capitalism also helped to feed, clothe and supply the domestic needs of a growing and increasingly urbanised population. Through its control over credit, it helped to 'provide a valuable, if imperfect, social service by financing working class people through periods of unemployment or low earnings'.[97] This army of anonymous working-class street traders, beerhouse proprietors and corner shop owners remained important, though still unduly neglected, representatives of nineteenth-century British capitalism.

11

Conclusion

The essence of penny capitalism lies in its elusiveness: it is difficult to define, harder still to identify, and virtually impossible to quantify. Thus it is hardly surprising that historians of all persuasions have tended to overlook penny capitalism (and other small-scale production) and sought instead to explore the development of large-scale capitalist enterprise. Yet however sensible this ordering of priorities may appear at first sight, it has had most unfortunate consequences: for it has resulted in a view of nineteenth and early-twentieth-century Britain which, if not incorrect, is most certainly incomplete. It would be easy, of course, to make excessively grandiose claims for the importance of penny capitalism. But even now, at this early stage of research, the study of penny capitalism does challenge many of the assumptions commonly made about economic growth and about working-class life.

One of the central purposes of this book has been to challenge the view that penny capitalism was destroyed by the growing forces of industrialisation, urbanisation and large-scale capitalism and to argue instead that it remained an important component of Victorian and Edwardian economic and social life. Unfortunately this hypothesis is easier to illustrate than it is to prove. There are two main difficulties, both of which — though common to all historical inquiry — become particularly acute when examining a little-known, sometimes illegal, and generally part-time activity such as penny capitalism. The first difficulty, that of classification, has already been discussed. Penny capitalists are not easy to identify: often they combined penny capitalism with wage labour; they moved from one form of penny capitalism to another and from penny capitalism to wage labour and back again. They merged with the wage labourers below and with the petty bourgeoisie above. The second difficulty arises from the fact that the more recent and more successful any historical activity, the more evidence of it is likely to survive. Thus what might seem to the historian to be convincing evidence of the survival of penny capitalism in full vigour may represent only a growing volume of evidence about what was in fact a stagnant or declining form of economic activity.

Nonetheless, if it cannot be shown that penny capitalism survived intact into the twentieth century, it can certainly be demonstrated that it was not destroyed by the centripetal forces of urban and industrial development. Naturally precision is impossible, but what little statistical evidence there is offers convincing support for the view that penny capitalism remained a widespread and vital component of working-class life throughout the nineteenth and early twentieth centuries. The only detailed statistical evidence comes from Elizabeth Roberts' fascinating oral investigation of working-class life in Barrow, Lancaster and Preston between 1890 and 1930. This study is of crucial importance. A careful analysis of her evidence reveals that despite the considerable physical, economic, industrial, political and demographic differences between the three towns, in each case between forty and forty four per cent of working-class families engaged in some form of penny capitalist activity at some time between 1890 and 1914.[1]

Of course it is not sufficient simply to count the number of families who engaged for some time (however short) in some form of penny capitalist activity (however trivial). After all, there were enormous differences in ambition, investment, commitment, and not least vulnerability, between, for example, the man who one year decided to sell a few vegetables from his allotment and the widow with young children who staked the whole of her family's future on the success of a tiny parlour shop. It is necessary to move beyond the mere counting of penny capitalist heads towards some assessment of the importance of this varied form of enterprise.

Immediately it is essential to distinguish between two types of penny capitalist: the person who, while retaining other sources of income, tried to make a little money on the side; and the person who went into business with the express intention, at least in the long term, of attaining independence of wage labour. Often of course the distinction becomes blurred; but it is important nonetheless. Part-time penny capitalism was essentially defensive. It was one of the strategies adopted by working people to meet immediate financial needs and to cope with the persistent, nagging poverty brought about by underemployment. More often than not, it was intended to prevent things getting worse, rather than to make things get better. Consequently part-time penny capitalism was always most common among the most disadvantaged. Like petty crime, with which it was often closely linked, it was typically the resort of women and children, the casually employed and the unskilled.[2]

The working-class family experienced its most extreme hardship just before the eldest child left school to go to work. It was at this stage that there were young children to bring up, that the mother was tied to the home, and that expenses weighed most heavily against wages. It was at this stage that the elder boys were most likely to take to petty crime and/or street-selling. Probably many boys needed but little encouragement to try to boost the family income. Indeed it is paradoxical that the extension of compulsory education together with the increasingly severe restrictions being placed upon children's employment may actually have encouraged penny capitalism among young people by excluding them from more normal, waged employment.[3] It was at this stage too that the husband might well obtain an allotment; at this stage that the wife began to undertake a home-based craft or personal service which it was possible to combine with her domestic commitments. In Barrow, Lancaster and Preston between forty and forty two per cent of working-class mothers engaged in some form of part-time penny capitalist activity after marriage — although, most strikingly, only one of the women had ever been a penny capitalist while single.[4] Naturally these part-time jobs were exhausting. There was the wife of a Barrow maintenance man earnings 25s. a week who had seven children but still found the time to go out washing, to take in washing, and to keep pigs. Then there was the widow of a Preston bricklayer who brought up eight children, went cleaning, took in lodgers and ran a small shop. Exhaustion was almost beside the point however. There was little to lose: because these part-time penny capitalist activities could be fitted into the working-class wife's 'free' time, almost any income (even if not profit in the strict economic sense) constituted an acceptable return on the modest capital invested and on the heavy (but uncosted) labour expended.[5]

Full-time and nearly full-time penny capitalism was very different. Here entry was determined, not so much by self-defence, as by the desire to attain independence from wage labour. Even the majority of these worker capitalists who had no desire to rise out of their class certainly wished to rise economically within it. Another difference was that full and almost full-time penny capitalism tended to be the domain, not of women, children and the unskilled, but of middle-aged, skilled, male artisans and other workers who had managed to save some money. It was part of their mid-life search for independence, for freedom from the increasingly severe restraints of factory and other work discipline.[6] Paradoxically, then, penny capitalism could represent the rejection, rather than the acceptance, of industrial capitalism. Still another difference from part-time penny capitalism was that it was at once much less common, yet much less uniform. Again the evidence comes overwhelmingly from turn of the century Barrow, Lancaster and Preston where, it will be recalled, the number of working-class mothers engaged in part-time penny capitalism remained constant at between forty and forty two per cent. The proportion of their husbands dependent upon penny capitalism as their chief source of income varied greatly: from as low as nought per cent in the Lancaster sample, to eight per cent in Barrow (nine per cent in Birmingham) and up to as high as eleven per cent in Preston.[7]

While it is not surprising that the popularity of full-time and nearly full-time penny capitalism should lag behind that of part-time, it is not entirely clear why it was subject to such wide variation. It seems however, that the explanation is to be sought in the varied nature of nineteenth and early-twentieth-century local economies. Full-time penny capitalism was found in three distinct types of economy. One type was that in which a high proportion of women worked full-time, a situation likely both to encourage ambitious husbands to take the risk of abandoning wage labour and to drive those without a job towards penny capitalism. This would be consistent with — and might help to explain — the high incidence of apparently full-time penny capitalism in textile towns like Preston, where nearly a third of all women were in full-time employment in 1901.[8]

Far more influential in determining the incidence and nature of such male penny capitalism was the openness of the local economic structure. The system of landholding could be important. Fragmented ownership tended to encourage — or at least did little to discourage — penny capitalist activity. Thus it was found in Blackpool that the absence of a single, large landlord who might have enforced restrictive clauses in leases made it difficult to prevent the spread of stalls and fairgrounds onto private land. Important, too, were working-class perceptions of the local economy. Places like Birmingham, Sheffield and parts of London, where small enterprises were at the centre of the local economy, encouraged skilled artisans to view their own industry as a vehicle for escaping from reliance upon wage labour. Geoffrey Crossick saw this process at work in mid-century Kentish London. 'A high turnover of firms, such as occurred in building and in small metal work, encourages a view of the openness of economic opportunity, however much actual mobility may in practice deny it for the overwhelming majority of even the skilled working class.'[9]

On the other hand, in heavily capitalised industries such as coal-mining, iron-making, or shipbuilding it was virtually impossible for any workman, however ambitious and talented, to begin work on his own account — and difficult too for women to get work. Yet even in this type of expanding, though unstable, local economy, the penny capitalist drive was not stifled but redirected away from production and manufacturing towards the tertiary sector — a movement which in all probability was reinforced by the increasingly unwelcome control which large employers were exercising over their workers.[10]

In areas dependent upon fishing, farming, building or

handicrafts, the full-time or nearly full-time male penny capitalist was likely to be a fisherman, farmer, builder or craftworker; in areas dependent upon heavy industry, he was likely to be some sort of shopkeeper. Thus what little is known about the existence, type and extent of full-time penny capitalism suggests that it was related to local economic circumstances rather than to any real, or perceived, stage in the development of capitalism proper.

Unlike the part-time worker capitalist, the man dependent upon penny capitalism had to try to be economically 'rational' for he could not rest content with any income, no matter how tiny. His investment was both too large and too small: too large to allow him to abandon his enterprise when things grew difficult; too small to enable him to break out of the strait-jacket of undercapitalisation and overproduction and develop into a true capitalist. Mayhew, it will be recalled, identified the dilemma only too clearly when examining the garret-masters in the East End cabinet trade: 'it is well known how strong is the stimulus among peasant-proprietors, or indeed any class working for themselves, to extra production' and thus to lower prices.[11] Moreover the difficulties were increasing. For although penny capitalists were not over-concerned with the letter of the law (and some prohibitive legislation such as that against Sunday drinking actually stimulated activity), the growing number of bye-laws concerning buildings, the employment of children and the obstruction of the streets did become burdensome. In 1895, for example, Edward Burke, a marine store dealer from Crewe, was summoned for erecting a shed in his yard for use as a workshop without first submitting the necessary plans to the Borough Surveyor.[12] In the Darwinian jungle of nineteenth and early-twentieth-century penny capitalism the number of rags to riches stories was very small. Penny capitalism, whether full or part-time, should be associated not with prosperity, but with marginality.

It is no easy matter to assess the contribution which penny capitalism made towards the economic development of modern Britain. Although there is no lack of theoretical guidance from economists concerned with self-employment and the informal economy today, this is not always directly relevant to the evaluation of penny capitalism seventy years and more ago. Nonetheless, it is almost certainly from the work of development and other economists that it will be possible eventually to measure the impact which penny capitalism had upon the Victorian and Edwardian economy.[13] For the moment, it is possible to suggest only the probable scale and direction of that impact. It is true that penny capitalism was sometimes conducted by barter and so may have retarded the full development of a money economy. It is also true that it did almost nothing to alter the existing pattern of economic and social relations within the community. Yet there can be no doubt that on the whole penny capitalism acted as a buttress and a stimulus to the industrialisation process. In the first place, it provided employment and income in a very large minority of working-class families. The statistical evidence, restricted though it is, shows that even at the beginning of the present century penny capitalism constituted the chief support of up to ten per cent of all working-class families and the partial support of at least forty per cent. This contributed of course towards the growth of working-class purchasing power. But it had another result: precisely because it did not disrupt existing relations in the community, it helped to ease the dislocation caused by rapid economic and social change.[14]

The second way in which penny capitalism bolstered industrialisation was by the assistance which it afforded the restructuring of the economy. As in the Third World today, penny capitalists and other small entrepreneurs moved into the gaps left by large-scale, capital-intensive, mass production industry. As the economy changed, so small builders and craftsmen moved into repair; 'wee pawns' met the needs of those neglected by pawnbrokers proper; street traders moved into districts without shops; and drinking dens opened when and where there was a dearth of legal establishments.[15]

The final way in which penny capitalism contributed towards economic development was by its production of goods and services. Again, however, it is difficult to be precise. For even if it proves possible to apply to Victorian and Edwardian Britain the techniques used to measure the informal economy today, this will still leave unsolved the problem of determining the role within the informal economy of penny capitalism itself. It is clear already, however, that penny capitalism did make a significant contribution towards meeting local demands for primary and secondary products and, increasingly, for a whole range of services. More and more the penny capitalist, like other workers, came to be found at the place of service rather than at the place of production; more and more he helped to ease the emergence of the modern, industrial economy.

Among the many facets of life affected by penny capitalism, four stand out: the working-class family, class consciousness, economic and social mobility and working-class organisation. It is not surprising that the study of penny capitalism, which was so often home based, should reaffirm the central role of the family. It confirms the continuing economic importance of the family as a unit of production and of service as well as one simply of consumption. It confirms too that in their traditional, 'female' roles women continued to play a crucial, though still neglected, part in the economic life both of their families and of their localities. Indeed it is ironic that it should have been such traditional, domestic tasks which offered working-class women one of their few opportunities for greater emancipation. In its part-time form, however, female penny capitalism rarely resulted in much more than domestic tension. The woman taking in washing, sewing or lodgers probably became even more tired than usual and her husband even more irritable. Anything more ambitious could produce still greater resentment. When a working-class woman went into business on a full-time or almost full-time basis, the change in the economic balance of the marriage and the possible reversal of roles could lead to serious difficulties. On some occasions, as in the seaside accommodation industry, the wife was able to set herself up independently and break away from an unloved husband. Some men, presumably, were only too happy to live off their wives but others — most often perhaps in mining and heavy industrial areas where working women were a relatively unfamiliar sight — found themselves unable to cope with their loss of status and turned for comfort to drink.[16]

Whether conducted by the wife, by the husband or by

both, any family business — especially one on the margins of profitability — was likely to become a tyranny, extorting from its owners huge demands of both time and effort. The longed-for independence was likely to prove illusory, creating tension and discouraging the children from following their parents' example. A Kent man recalls that his carrier father bought a small farm in 1892, only to be ruined by a lack of rain. The son turned his back on such 'independence' and joined the navy: 'I says to him, look here, you worked hard all your life and what have you got for it now?'[17] Nonetheless the dream of independence — and of survival — remained potent; and the study of penny capitalism shows that the family, with the wife to the fore, continued to play a much greater role in economic life than is generally realised.

The study of penny capitalism has other implications. It throws further doubt, for example, on what has been described as 'one of the most commonly accepted notions in the economic and social history of late Victorian and Edwardian England . . . that the working people were slowly but assuredly being moulded into a homogeneous working class which enjoyed a common work experience and outlook'.[18] Penny capitalism was inimical to the development of a homogeneous working class. It added yet another layer to the already divisive forces of occupation, earnings, sex, nationality, geography, age, religious belief and racial identity. It divided the forty per cent of part-time penny capitalists and more particularly the ten per cent of full-time and nearly full-time penny capitalists from their neighbours who depended upon wage labour and other sources of income. Even the most modest enterprise might encourage its owner in the belief that his success or failure depended on his own efforts and that he and his family had a stake, however slight, in the existing economic and social system. Such, at least, was the middle and upper-class hope. The Select Committee on the Labouring Poor concluded in 1843 that even 'the system of garden allotments has proved an unmixed good . . . It gives him [the labourer] a stake in the country, and places him in the class which has something to lose.'[19] In fact, the greater the marginality of the penny capitalist, the more tenacious his adherence to the individualistic ideology was perhaps likely to become.

All this is far removed from the tidy generalisations of the text-book and does little to support the view that the class structure was becoming more simplified as the nineteenth century progressed. Even more inimical to the argument in favour of the development of an increasingly homogeneous working class would be the identification of any significant degree of upward social or economic mobility. It is clear of course that the forty per cent of working-class families engaged in part-time penny capitalism neither sought, nor achieved, upward mobility. Their ambitions were more modest: to retain what they had, or at least to diminish their losses. But what of the ten per cent who went into penny capitalism on a full-time or nearly full-time basis? Here the problem is more complex. One essential part of a Liberal view of the world is the belief in a 'ladder of opportunity' for those with the personal attributes to climb it. Others see this belief as a delusion of the cruelest kind. To Marxists, of course, the only economic mobility of any consequence during the nineteenth century was the downward mobility of the 'intermediate strata', the small independents in agriculture, manufacturing or trade, who were driven into the proletariat by their lack of capital and by their inability to withstand new methods of production.[20]

It is not easy to arrive at the truth of the matter so far as penny capitalists are concerned. On the one hand, it is important not to overlook the existence of a few successful full-time penny capitalists who made enough money to move close economically to the petty bourgeoisie, with whom they explored the same possibilities, shared the same worries, and earned a similar sort of living. In late-nineteenth-century Oldham, for example, fifteen of the eighty seven employers and professional men identified by John Foster came from manual-working-class backgrounds. On the other hand, it is essential not to exaggerate the extent of such economic mobility, confined as it was to but a tiny proportion of the ten per cent of families (at most) who depended chiefly upon penny capitalism.

Nor is there any reason to suppose that even those most upwardly mobile in economic terms came to adopt middle-class values and attitudes — rather the reverse. The low and uncertain income of all but a handful of full-time penny capitalists made it difficult to adopt a middle-class life-style, even if this was desired. Nor did full-time penny capitalism always appear quite respectable. For one thing, it was often born of unemployment; for another, it was often linked with criminality. Penny capitalism, it is essential to remember, was frequently viewed as downward — rather than upward — social mobility.[21] In all events, even full-time penny capitalists retained intimate links with their working-class background. They lived among their working-class relatives, friends and customers. They retained the collective, communal and mutually supportive aspects of working-class life: coster-mongers, for example, collected for colleagues whose donkeys had died, and even when a workman became a small master employing one or two men he did not necessarily leave the artisan world, nor abandon his trade-union membership. Nor is this surprising when it is remembered that, for those employed in manufacturing industry, entry into penny capitalism often arose in part from a desire to retain a working-class life-style against the incursions of the employers. In many respects then such a move represented a rejection, rather than an acceptance, of conventional capitalist values. Like labour aristocrats, full-time penny capitalists might appear to adopt middle-class values, but they often did so through institutions which were characteristically working class. Even the illusory nature of the 'ladder of opportunity' cannot obscure the fact that the examination of penny capitalism offers little comfort to those who seek to identify the development of an increasingly homogeneous working class during the nineteenth and early-twentieth centuries.[22]

The heterogeneity encouraged by penny capitalism had implications for working-class political and industrial organisation. Middle-class observers hoped, and social critics feared, that the divisions which penny capitalism engendered within the working class, like the mobility which it was supposed to encourage out of it, would soften antagonisms between capital and labour. As Dr Blaikie told his Edinburgh audience in 1866, 'By becoming themselves capitalists, and in a sense masters, workmen will be in a much better position to understand the merits of the questions that are so fiercely agitated between employers and employed.'[23] A few years later Kay-Shuttleworth reassured his Lancashire listeners – and no doubt himself – that, 'The knowledge that a skilful, prudent man may accumulate from his earnings the means of building cottages, or entering into a retail trade, or into some business requiring greater intelligence and energy, or even into the wide field of manufacturing enterprise, makes the success of the middle classes less a subject of envy than of emulation.'[24] Even at the very end of the period it was possible for an informed commentator to remark on 'the obvious fact which rose to the eyes that the vertical mobility of labour was removing the possibility of class hatred by a continual fusion of classes'.[25]

Such observations had some validity in the case of the few full-time penny capitalists. The intense competition common to all forms of working-class entrepreneurial activity naturally made this a difficult group to organise. Even late in the century trade unions in both cab driving and hairdressing had to accommodate movement between employers and employees, while union organisers in the Sheffield cutlery trades were still complaining about working-class 'little masters' who 'undermine the Union and of course reduce the price of labour'.[26] Yet at the same time full-time penny capitalism did allow its practitioners to be politically and socially independent, and sometimes of course was undertaken for this very reason. Thus when the Durham coal-mining trade unionist, John Wilson, was blacklisted in the 1870s he and his family took over a small shop between Durham City and Hartlepool. As the daughter of a penny capitalist in rural Kent points out, 'You see all the farm labourers, they used to have to vote Conservative or else they'd get the sack. So they was really tied to their masters in those days. But my dad was his own master . . .'[27] Indeed, it has been argued that thwarted 'expectations of just economic reward were and are a major factor in class action'[28] and that 'so heavy were the disabilities upon their personal initiatives that when the manual workers thought to challenge the system they turned naturally to state action'.[29]

The political and industrial consequences of part-time penny capitalism were equally complex. On the one hand, they weakened the workers' position by helping to sustain a pool of labour ready for use by the employers in labour shortages or during industrial disputes and, it was claimed, by channelling working-class energies away from dangerous interests such as politics. A Hinckley witness reassured the Select Committee on the Labouring Poor in 1843 that 'one of the lecturers of the Chartists, from Leicester, came there a week or two ago, and made a great noise, but none of the allotment tenants visited him; instead of going to the meeting, they went with their spades on their shoulders to their gardens'.[30] On the other hand, part-time penny capitalism also furthered independent working-class action. Although not the type of activity likely to be drawn attention to before parliamentary (or other) inquiries, it was important for all that. It provided practical experience of organisation, may have encouraged self-confidence, and did something at least to mitigate the poverty brought about by industrial disputes. This is really little more than conjecture and for the moment, therefore, the impact of penny capitalism upon working-class political and industrial organisation must remain an open question.

Such a tentative conclusion may stand, in one sense, as an epitaph for the whole of the book. As this final chapter has made clear, research into penny capitalism is still very much at the pioneering stage. But it is hoped that this, the first full length study of penny capitalism, has identified some important issues, provided some interesting evidence and suggested some sensible answers. If it succeeds in drawing attention to its subject, in stimulating further inquiry and in goading other historians into challenging the views expressed here, it will have achieved its purpose.

Notes

INTRODUCTION
1 Benson (1980), 89-90.
2 Payne (1974), 34; Samuel (1975), xiii-xxi.
3 Schmiechen (1975), 413. Also Markovitch (1970), 229.
4 Boswell (1973), 42.
5 Benson (1980), 1-5.
6 See, for example, Anderson (1971), Stedman Jones (1971), Samuel (1975) and Humphries (1981).
7 Roberts (1977) and Samuel (1975).
8 Tax (1953). Cf. Vincent (1963—4), 82 who refers to '"urban peasants" — self-employed men and small capitalists in overalls'. For criticism of this usage, see Mills (1980), 44. Cf. Scott (1979).
9 Bythell (1978), 38.
10 Wilson (1957), 103; Payne (1974), 14.
11 Crossick (1977), 15. Also Marglin (1974), 16; Crossick (1979); Bythell (1978), 14 and White (1980), 260.
12 Editorial Collective (1977), 4.
13 Schmiechen (1975), 413.

THE PRIMARY SECTOR:
MINING AND FISHING
1 *Fish Trades Gazette*, 18 Aug 1883; University of Kent Oral History Project (hereafter Kent), G2, 193; Samuel (1977), 8, 23-4.
2 Calvert (1915), 631. Also Samuel (1977), 166-9.
3 Samuel (1977), 22-3. Also Raistrick and Jennings (1965), 257-9; Fairbairn (1980), 245.
4 Howarth (1978), 81.
5 Williams (1962), 654-5.
6 Grant (1977), 270-1; Benson (1980), 22, 62; Harrison (1978).
7 Kent, G5, 21-2, 24, 27.
8 Carpenter (1975); Winstanley (1978), 148-56.
9 Rule (1973), 60. Also *Fish Trades Gazette*, 23 June 1883; *Fishing News*, 14 April 1913; M'Iver (1906), 51, 278; Marsh (c.1952), 174; Tunstall (1962), 17-19.
10 Kent, P11, 9. Also D2, 4; University of Lancaster Oral History Project (hereafter Lancaster), P1B, 3-4; *Aberdeen Journal*, 10, 17 May

1877; *Sandbach Guardian*, 20 Feb 1895; *Fishing News*, 16 May, 27 June 1913; Lawson (1944), 25-6.

11 *Census*, 1891—1921. For a discussion of the reliability of this evidence see *Census*, 1891, *General Report*, 36.

12 Kent, D2, 19. Also P11, 15.

13 Kent, P11, 11, 13, 36. Also D2, 23; Douglas (n.d.), 16.

14 Kent, P11, 12, 36; D2, 10; Leather (1971), 61.

15 Lancaster, M1B, 8; M1L, 55; Kent, D2, 12; P11, 17; *Fish Trades Gazette*, 16 June, 14 July 1883; Rule (1973), 55; Winstanley (1978), 102, 130.

16 Kent, P11, 30. Also 4, 17, 30; D2, 2; M4, 117; Marsh (c.1952), 244; Rule (1973), 61-2.

17 *Fish Trades Gazette*, 14 July 1883. Also Rule (1976), 130-1.

18 Kent, P11, 54; Leather (1971), 62; Marsh (c.1952), 182; Tunstall (1962), 23.

19 *Fish Trades Gazette*, 10 Nov 1883. Also 2, 9, 23 June, 4 Aug 1883; *Fishing News*, 9, 16 May 1913; Kent, P11, 9.

20 Kent, M4, 115-6. Also Mayhew (1861—2), II, 147; Leather (1971), 53.

21 Winstanley (1978), 105.

22 Lancaster, Mrs D1P, 59.

FARMING

1 Levy (1911), 217; *Report from the Select Committee on Small Holdings*, 1889, Q. 8,096, R B Haldane.

2 Samuel (1977), 142-3, 191. Also Orwin and Wheltham (1964), 205.

3 Kent, M4, 105.

4 Jebb (1907), 247-8. Also Benson (1980), 78-9; *Report of the Departmental Committee of Inquiry into Allotments*, 1969, 7; Davies (1909), 135-6; Lancaster A2L, 64; M1B, 79.

5 Lancaster, M1L, 55.

6 Samuel (1977), 198.

7 Kent, M7, 22. Also *The Smallholder*, 24 Dec 1910.

8 Lancaster, M1B, 13. Also Mr D2P, 24; Kent, B8, 130; S10, 3.

9 Gresswell (1956), 46-7.

10 Lancaster, A3B, 10. Also Kent, G2, 96-7; M4, 8-9; S10, 14-15; V1, 33, 103; Orwin and Wheltham (1964), 211; Constantine (1981), 393.

11 *Returns of the Number of Allotments detached from and attached to Cottages . . .*, 1886, 7-8; *Report Departmental Committee*, 1969, 5, 7; Lord Fortescue (1888), 397; Green (1896), 90; Ashby (1917), 3, 88-9.

12 Foster (1974), 84; Cunningham (1980), 81-2; Constantine (1981), 394.

13 *S C Small Holdings*, 1889, Q. 3,527-3,726; *Report Departmental Committee*, 1969, 10-12, 47; Roberts (1981), 17-18; Roberts (1978), 186; *The Smallholder*, 24 Sep 1910; Rowntree (1902),

113; Bowley and Hurst (1915), 81; Thorpe (1975), 170-2; Samuel (1975), 192.

14 Samuel (1975), 190, 197-8. Also Lancaster, J1L, 28; Ashby (1974), 126.

15 Lancaster, M1B, 37.

16 *The Smallholder*, 6 Aug 1910. Also Kent, M4, 107; B10, 14; G2, 137; Davies (1909), 106; Levy (1911), 165.

17 Lancaster, P2B, 5-6.

18 Norfolk Federation of Women's Institutes (1972), 13. Also Kent, B10, 22; V1, 4-5.

19 Samuel (1975), 193. Also Norfolk Federation of Women's Institutes (1972), 17; Kent, B10, 32; Gresswell (1956), 19-20, 39.

20 Williams (1915), 123, 159, 246. Also Sturt (1907), 14-15; Kent, B10, 32.

21 *The Smallholder*, 14 May 1910; Lancaster, Mr G1P, 18; Mr T1P, 34; Kent, V1, 35-6, 38; Hollingshead (1861), 137; Kenney (1939), 15-16; Samuel (1981), 14, 16; Langley (n.d.), 12; Forman (1979), 193-5.

22 Holdenby (1913), 189. Also *The Smallholder*, 22 Oct 1910; Kenney (1939), 59; Haggard (1975), 156-7; Ashby (1917), 43; Levy (1911), 178.

23 Mrs Bayly (1860), 30-31. Also Malcolmson (1975), 34; Barnsby (1980), 89.

24 Lancaster, H2B, 33. Also H1B, 16; Kent, M4, 110; Malcolmson (1975), 35-6; de Rousiers (1860), 22.

25 Gresswell (1956), 70-2.

26 Lancaster, J1L, 28. Also Mr G1P, 20; Kent, A1, 8. Of course what seem casual sales to old people recalling their childhood may in fact have been methods carefully thought out by their parents.

27 Lancaster, M1B, 80.

28 *The Smallholder*, 2 April 1910.

29 Lancaster, C1L, 20. Also Levy (1911), 175.

30 Jebb (1907), 54-5. Also Lancaster, H1B, 1; J1L, 28; M1B, 59, 82; Kent, B10, 47-8; G2, 160-1; V1, 36.

31 Green (1896), 32-3. Also Ashby (1917), 67; Orwin and Wheltham (1964), 89.

32 Lancaster, W1B, 4. Also Ashby (1917), 38.

33 Somerville (1848), 52. Also Kent, B10, 45; Orwin and Wheltham (1964), 222, 230.

34 Lancaster, M1L, 55. Also Mrs D1P, 67; Kent, G2, 10; S10, 77; Rowntree and Kendall (1913), 86-7, 99.

35 Kitchen (1940), 22. Also Samuel (1975), 198; Rowntree and Kendall (1913), 256-7.

36 Read (1887), 12.

37 Kent, V1, 106.

38 Read (1887), 35. Also Davies (1909), 130-1; Rowntree and Kendall (1913), 92.

39 Levy (1911), 178.

40   *The Smallholder*, 12 March 1910.
41   Samuel (1975), 199. Also Kent, B10, 29; Lancaster, H1B, 16.
42   Rowntree and Kendall (1913), 161-2.
43   Jebb (1907), 251, 255. Also 247-8.
44   Davies (1909), 112.
45   Holdenby (1913), 256. Also Rowntree and Kendall (1913), 331.
46   Holdenby (1913), 68, 80. Also Levy (1911), 215; Jebb (1907), 174.
47   Holdenby (1913), 250.
48   Kent, B10, 23; *S C Small Holdings*, 1889, Q. 2,854-6, W Holman; Bennett (1914), 169-70; Harris (1882), 8; Mills (1980), 102-3.
49   Holdenby (1913), 34, 114.
50   Kent, K1, 7. Also G2, 187; *The Smallholder*, 12 Nov 1910.
51   Jebb (1907), 103, 109. Also *Report from Select Committee on Labouring Poor (Allotments of Land)*, 1843, Q. 882-7, T Punt; *S C Small Holdings*, 1889, Q. 917, J Collings.
52   Udale (1908), 95. Also Jebb (1907), 57.
53   Ashby (1917), 9. Also 10, 77, 160; *S C Small Holdings*, 1889, Q. 739, J Collings; Springall (1936), 103.
54   Jebb (1907), 230-1; Garrett (1930), 74; Springall (1936), 125; Orwin and Wheltham (1964), 322.
55   *The Smallholder*, 12 March 1910; Jebb (1907), 104; Levy (1911), 97, 107; Ashby (1917), 88-9; Garrett (1930), 110-12.
56   Levy (1911), 106-7, 161.
57   Rowntree (1902), 192. Also *The Smallholder*, 2 April 1910; *S C Small Holdings*, 1889, Q. 3,366-71, G Wimpenny; Kent, B10, 24; Davies (1909), 262.
58   Holdenby (1913), 253. Also *S C Small Holdings*, 1889, Q. 2,615-58, W Dalton; Manchester Polytechnic Oral History Project (hereafter Manchester), 708; Lancaster, Mr A2L, 136; Samuel (1975), 8.
59   Ashby (1917), 171.
60   Levy (1911), 107 n.1. See too *The Smallholder*, 28 May, 3 Dec 1910; Lancaster, M1B, 80; Kent, K1, 48-9; Orwin and Wheltham (1964), 362.
61   Levy (1911), 165, 175. Also Ashby (1917), 129, 172; Bear (1908), 35; Kent, G2, 150.
62   Jebb (1907) 409-10. Also *The Smallholder*, 2 April 1910; Bear (1908), 35; Kent, G2, 150.
63   Holdenby (1913), 271. Also Stirton (1894), 92; Levy (1911), 189.
64   Ashby (1917), 95. See also *The Smallholder*, 17 Sep 1910; Kent, C17, 1; Blackman (1963), 93; Chambers and Mingay (1966), 38, 106.
65   Ashby (1974), 5.
66   Williams (1915), 296.
67   Chambers and Mingay (1966), 106-7.
68   Green (1896), 90-1. Also *The Smallholder*, 12 March 1910; Bennett (1914), 170.
69   Levy (1911), 154; Mingay (1968), 13; Jones (1968), 19.
70   Read (1887), 10, 22. Also Hobsbawm and Rudé (1973), 16-17.

THE SECONDARY SECTOR:
MANUFACTURING

1 Hanson (1884), 20; Chapman and Marquis (1912), 299; Bythell (1978), 30.

2 Checkland (1964), 219; Foster (1974), 9-13; Bythell (1978), 30-2, 44.

3 *Report from the Select Committee on Manufactures, Commerce and Shipping*, 1833, Q. 5,302, H Houldsworth. Also Q. 5,303; Gatrell (1977), 124-5.

4 I am grateful to Dr D A Farnie for this reference.

5 Samuel (1977a), 8.

6 Kent, T4, 52. Also S10, 92; Kenney (1939), 50-1; Hartley and Ingilby (1969), 28.

7 Lancaster, A3B, 24. Also *The Smallholder*, 2 July 1910; Thomson and Smith (1877–8), 73; Davies (1908), 209; Samuel (1977a), 17, 26.

8 *Report from Select Committee on the Sale of Beer*, 1833, Q. 2,203, W Thurnall; Glen (1970), 78; Devine (1975); Williams (1976), 74-5.

9 Bundy and Healy (1978), 89. See also *Pawnbrokers' Gazette*, 29 Sep 1900; Lipman (1959), 67-8; Hall (1962), 54; Alexander (1970), 136-42; Richards (1974), 352; Meacham (1977), 83.

10 Lancaster, D3P, 18.

11 Lancaster, Mrs M6B, 71.

12 Lancaster; Rowntree and Kendall (1913), 199; Bythell (1978), 66, 70.

13 *The Tailor*, 22 Dec 1866. Also Kent, B3, 6; Lancaster C2P, 9; D2P, 45; Williams (1915), 39; Hamilton (1978), 81; Samuel (1972), 7.

14 Davies (1975), 104. Also Hall (1962), 145; Foster (1974), 297 n.19; Griffiths (1978 or 9), 7; Samuel (1977), 36; information from Geoff Crossick.

15 Williams (1915), 176. Also *The Smallholder*, 11 June 1910; Davies (1975), 156.

16 Information from Edmund Frow; de Rousiers (1896), 104; White (1980), 217; Behagg (1980); More (1980), 45; *S C Manufactures*, 1833, Q. 1,961-4, A Fretwell; Q. 2,862-3, S Jackson; Q. 4,663-8, T C Salt; Q. 11,604, J Milner.

17 Manchester, 592; Cooper (1971), 8-9, 12, 28; Philips (1977), 231-2. On London cabinetmaking see Mayhew (1861–2), II, 228-9; Hall (1962), 82, 86, 93; Samuel (1981), 5, 29, 94-8.

18 Meyer and Black (1909), 141. Also 90; *The Tailor*, 6 April 1867; Lancaster, C2P, 9; Lipman (1959), 6; Hall (1962), 59, 63-4, 119; Williams (1976), 44; Jefferys (1954), 333; Williams (1979), 47.

19 Booth (1892), I, 34, 56.

20 Mayhew (1861–2), II, 332. Also 228; III, 223; *S C Manufactures*, 1833, Q. 4,369-71, J Dixon; Kent, D6, 9; Lancaster, M6B, 71; Goodman (1968), 88; de Rousiers (1896), 100; Foster (1974), 175.

21　Meyer and Black (1909), 90.
22　Lancaster, Mr D2P, 41. Also *S C Manufactures*, 1833, Q. 4,370-6, 4,474, J Dixon; Q. 4,654, 4,669, T C Salt; Foster (1974), 175-6.
23　*The Tailor*, 24 Nov 1866.
24　Crossick (1978), 81, 163.
25　Webbs (1913), 546. Also *Royal Commission on Labour, 2nd Report*, 1893, Q. 19,018, 19,075, C Hobson.
26　Behagg (1980); Samuel (1981), 102. But see Williams (1976), 274.

BUILDING
1　Kenney (1939), 80. Also *Royal Commission on Friendly and Benefit Building Societies, 1st Report*, 1871, Q. 5,500, S Andrew; *Fish Trades Gazette*, 11 Aug 1883; Allen (1959), 295; Bowley (1966), 338-9; Dyos (1968), 664; Price (1980), 20.
2　Samuel (1975), 175. Also 174, 176.
3　Dyos (1968), 652. Also 651, 654, 659, 678; *Plumber and Decorator*, 1 Dec 1879; Burgess (1975), 90-2; Crossick (1978), 57-8.
4　Kenney (1939), 80-1. Also Stedman Jones (1971), 50.
5　Howarth and Wilson (1907), 11-12.
6　*Plumber and Decorator*, 1 Nov 1879. Also Price (1980), 23-4, 31.
7　Lancaster, N1L, 4.
8　Burgess (1975), 138; Price (1980), 21.
9　Hartwell (1973), 370.

THE TERTIARY SECTOR:
TRANSPORT
1　Hartwell (1973).
2　*Fish Trades Gazette*, 8 Sep 1883; *Hackney Carriage Guardian*, 12 June 1886; J Hicks to *Bexhill-on-Sea Chronicle*, 19 Nov 1887; Winstanley (1978), 99; Walton and McGloin (1981), 160, 174-5; Grass (1972), 18, 25.
3　*Articles of Agreement made between the Members of A Society . . .*, 1808; *Rules and Regulations of The Hope Iron Boat Club*, 1856; Willan (1964), 105; Wilson (1973), 3; Hanson (1975), 21-2, 37, 105, 107, 111, 123; Crossick (1978), 54.
4　Hanson (1975), 109. Also Crossick (1978), 63; Samuel (1977), 150-1; Mayhew (1861—2), II, 137, 328-33; *Sandbach Guardian*, 6 Feb 1895.
5　Hanson (1975), 116-7. Also 26-7, 106-7, 113-5; Wilson (1973), 16; Crossick (1978), 54; *The Waterman*, Jan 1897.
6　Kent, T4, 14. Also *Hackney Carriage Guardian*, 12 June 1886; Anon (1876), 105; Common (1974), 147.
7　*Census*, 1891; *Road Journal*, 25 May 1889.
8　Thomson and Smith (1877—8), 5. Also *Hackney Carriage Guardian*, 7 Oct 1885; 3 April 1886; *Cab Trade Record*, Dec 1902.
9　Ashby (1917), 160. Also *Labour Tribune*, 3 May 1890.
10　Thompson (1976), 72, 80.
11　Ashby (1974), 11.

12 Everitt (1973), 229-30. Also Kent, C17, 1; Mayhew (1861—2), II, 287-8, 362-4; *Cab Trade Record*, Oct 1902; *The Smallholder*, 11 June 1910; Freeman (1914), 61; Samuel (1975), 176-9; Thompson (1976), 63, 71-2.

13 *Cab Trade Record*, Oct 1901.

14 *Hackney Carriage Guardian*, March, May 1884; 16 Jan, 12 June 1886; *Cab Trade Record*, Oct, Nov 1901; Jan, May 1902; Mayhew (1861—2), III, 351, 355; Thomson and Smith (1877—8), 6; Williams (1915), 236; Thompson (1976), 61.

16 Somerville (1848), 1. Also *Aberdeen Journal*, 30 April 1877; *Hackney Carriage Guardian*, March 1884.

17 *Hackney Carriage Guardian*, 1 May 1886; Samuel (1975), 204; Thompson (1976), 78.

18 *Cab Trade Record*, May 1902.

19 Hanson (1975), 10.

20 *Hackney Carriage Guardian*, 10 April 1886. Also 3 April 1886; *Centaur*, 3 May 1879; *Road Journal*, 27 April, 8 June, 20 July, 3 Aug 1889; *Cab Trade Record*, Sep 1901, Feb 1902.

21 *Hackney Carriage Guardian*, March 1884; *Cab Trade Record*, July 1902.

22 Ashby (1974), 218-9.

23 Kent, K1, 8. Also *Aberdeen Journal*, 26 April 1877; *Road Journal*, 27 April 1889; *Cab Trade Record*, Nov 1901; Thomson and Smith (1877—8), 5-6.

24 Thompson (1976), 61.

25 Chartres (1977), 81.

ENTERTAINMENT

1 Mayhew (1861—2), III, 44-6; *The Era*, 7 July 1900; Frost (1874), 320; Malcolmson (1973); Starsmore (1975), 16-17; Storch (1976), 483, 489; Cunningham (1980), 38, 51, 73, 106-7, 164-9, 184; Thompson (1981), 198, 200.

2 Cunningham (1980), 175.

3 *Report from the Select Committee on Theatres and Places of Entertainment*, 1892, Q. 4,152, A C Bruce. Also *The Magnet*, 12 April 1890; Mayhew (1861—2), III, 214-9; Frost (1874), 257, 303; Howell and Ford (1980), 27, 149; Samuel (1981), 35.

4 Lancaster, Mrs D1P, 28. Also Mr T3P, 44; Kent, B8, 126-7; *The Era*, 14 July 1900; Manchester, 486; Ord-Hume (1978), 250; Samuel (1981), 10.

5 *The Era*, 14, 21 July 1900. Also *The Bioscope*, 27 Nov, 10, 17, 24 Dec 1908; Chanan (1980), 17, 49, 258.

6 *The Bioscope*, 10 Dec 1908.

7 Lancaster, Mrs G2L, 12. Also *Sandbach Guardian*, 30 March 1895; *Photographic Work*, 6 Jan 1903; Mayhew (1861—2), III, 79-89; Chanan (1980), 22, 76, 101, 223, 234.

8 Samuel (1981), 33. Also *The Magnet*, 27 Jan 1900; *The Era*, 18 Aug 1900; Cunningham (1980), 174.

9   *The Era*, 1 Sep 1900.
10   Lancaster, Mrs M6B, 110. Also 4, 57, 70, 107; Mrs T1P, 24.
11   Mayhew (1861–2), IV, 214; Finnegan (1979), 14.
12   Mayhew (1861–2), IV, 230. Also McHugh (1980), 18.
13   Finnegan (1979), 69, 107-9, 112-13. Also Walkowitz (1977), 79.
14   *S C Sale of Beer*, 1833, Q. 2,262, P Townley; *Report from the Select Committee on Public Houses*, 1852–3, Q. 6,124, 6,127, Rev J Clay; *Report of Royal Commission upon the Administration and Operation of the Contagious Diseases Acts*, 1871, Q. 5,108, W Luscombe.
15   Mayhew (1861–2), IV, 264; Finnegan (1979), 104-7.
16   Storch (1976), 485, 487; Finnegan (1979), 109-12.
17   Samuel (1981), 91. Also 176, 281, 326; information from Elizabeth Roberts.
18   *Hairdresser's Weekly Journal*, 22 Jan 1910. See too Thompson (1977), 74.
19   *Report from the Select Committee of the House of Lords on Betting*, 1902, Q. 88, J Hawke; Q. 99, Earl of Durham; Q. 1,002, F W Spruce; Manchester, 653; Rowntree (1905), 26-7, 93-4; Miller (1974), 8-9; McKibbin (1979), 147-8, 159, 168-9.
20   *Report from the Select Committee of the House of Lords on Betting*, 1901, Q. 119, J Hawke; Q. 2,244, B Thomas; *S C Betting*, 1902, Q. 1,701, R Allen; Q. 1,366-70, J Sutters; Rowntree (1905), 93; Paterson (1911), 170; Miller (1974), 9, 12. Reliance on 'S P' odds could also cause the bookmaker difficulties by preventing him from balancing his liabilities.
21   Samuel (1981), 121. Also Miller (1974), 8-9.
22   *S C Betting*, 1901, Q. 7, J Hawke; 1902, Q. 156, R Peacock; Q. 1,747, Superintendent Shannon; Q. 1,366-70, J Sutters; McKibbin (1979), 147 n.2; Samuel (1981), 176.
23   McKibbin (1979), 172.
24   *S C Betting*, 1902, Q. 2,898-3,000, F W Tannett-Walker. Also Rowntree (1905), 94.
25   Miller (1974), 8, 50-1.
26   McKibbin (1979), 172.

PERSONAL SERVICES
1   Holman (1952), 90-1. Also Kent, S3, 9; Manchester, 797, 7.
2   Lancaster, Mr D2P, 25.
3   Manchester, 918; Riverside Visitor (1892), 122-3.
4   Kent, B3, 31.
5   Freeman (1914), 15-21, 29-40, 42-9, 55-7, 59-70; Roberts (1978), 311.
6   Malcolmson (1975), 40, 44-5. Also Samuel (1975), 179.
7   *Census*, 1911.
8   Lancaster, A2B, 103. Also Mrs D1P, 36, 38; N1L, 8; Mrs T3P, 10; Kent, S10, 15-18; Hostettler (1976), 16; Forman (1979), 132; Benson (1980), 124-5.

9 Kent, S3, 9.
10 Hunt (1981), 24.
11 Kent, M1, 15.
12 Davies (1909), 125. Also Kent, S10, 129; Lancaster, A2B, 103; A3B, 5; Mrs D1P, 1; Samuel (1981), 57.
13 Lancaster, W1B, 48.
14 Bundy and Healy (1978), 91. Also Davidoff (1979), 79-80.
15 *Pawnbrokers' Gazette*, 13 Jan, 3 Aug 1840; Manchester, 538, 14; 539, 1.
16 Kitchen (1940), 87. Also Kent, V1, 65; Anderson (1971), 46-7; Thompson (1977), 90; Roberts (1978), 50; Benson (1980), 123.
17 *Bexhill-On-Sea Chronicle*, 12 Nov 1887; *Census*, 1911; Bell (1907), 48; Anderson (1971), 46; Roberts (1977), 311; Walton (1978), 30, 96.
18 Loane (1908), 58-9. Also Kent, T5, 13-14; Bell (1907), 49; Bowley and Hurst (1915), 153; Anderson (1971), 47; Davidoff (1979), 83-4; Benson (1980), 123.
19 Lancaster, N1L, 55.
20 Walton (1978), 90. Also 80-5, 92, 110, 114; Lancaster, Mr 2DP, 1, 37; Kent, P3, 4, 26; S10, 69; Loane (1908), 58; Davies (1909), 135; *Census*, 1851—91; Sturt (1977), 226.
21 Kent, P3, 19-21. Also 4; Lancaster, Mr G1P, 35; T3P, 82; Winstanley (1978), 207; Walton (1978), 3-4; Davidoff (1979), 68-9.
22 Kent, P3, 1-5, 22; Lancaster, Mr G1P, 35; Bell (1907), 49; Walton (1978), 122-8, 133, 164.
23 Kent, P3, 2. Also 11, 17, 24; *Bexhill-On-Sea Chronicle*, 26 Nov 1887; Philips (1977), 197; Walton (1978), 73, 87, 99-102, 107-9, 112-13, 136; Davidoff (1979), 71.
24 Lancaster, Mrs M6B, 51, 106; Mrs O1P, 17; Barnes (1976), 131.
25 *Report from the Select Committee on Education of the Poorer Classes in England and Wales*, 1838, Q. 7-14, J P Kay; Q. 1,089, J R Wood; Q. 1,477, H Althans; *Report of the Commissioners appointed to inquire into the State of Popular Education in England*, 1861, 28-9, 92, 94; Sturt (1967), 38; Horn (1978), 15, 18; Wardle (1971), 148, 167; West (1975), 35; For an exception to the comments made in this paragraph see Leinster-Mackay (1976).
26 Horn (1978), 17. Also *State Popular Education*, 1861, 94; Leinster-Mackay (1976), 42-3; Wardle (1971), 167.
27 *State Popular Education*, 1861, 92. Also 93; *S C Education of the Poor*, 1838, Q. 1,241, J R Wood; Cooper (1971), 72-3; Colls (1976), 90; Horn (1978), 40; Higginson (1974), 178.
28 Leinster-Mackay (1976), 37.
29 *State Popular Education*, 1861, 95, 177; Whitbread (1972), 7; Horn (1978), 16.
30 McCann (1977), 29. Also Whitbread (1972), 24.
31 Leinster-Mackay (1976), 33, 45-6. Also Davies (1973), 38; *State Popular Education*, 1861, 95.
32 Leinster-Mackay (1976), 47; Horn (1976), 44.

33 *S C Education of the Poor*, 1838, Q. 1,477. H Altham. See too Wardle (1971), 166-8; Whitbread (1972), 7; Leinster-Mackay (1976), 38; Horn (1978), 23-5; Samuel (1975), 120-3.

34 *State Popular Education*, 1861, 92. Also Wardle (1971), 168; Leinster-Mackay (1976), 44; Horn (1978), 23.

35 *Colliery Guardian*, 30 Jan 1858.

36 Seeley (1973), 127; Kent, V1, 10-11, 85.

37 Kitchen (1940), 72. Also *The Tailor*, 23 Feb 1867; *The Small-holder*, 14 May 1910; Benson (1980), 89.

38 Greenwood (1967), 20.

39 *Hairdresser's Weekly Journal*, 30 Sep 1882. Also 23 Sep 1882; 1 Jan, 19 March, 4 April 1910; *The Hairdresser*, 15 Jan 1912.

40 *Report from the Select Committee on Sunday Trading (Metropolis)*, 1847, Q. 2,076, C James; Q. 2,103, W Carpenter.

41 Common (1938), 7.

42 *S C Sunday Trading*, 1847, Q. 1,544-5, A Rult; *S C Betting*, 1902, Q. 2,121, J Orr; Freeman (1914), 17; Paterson (1911), 105; Greenwood (1967), 59.

43 O'Mara (1934), 128. Also *Hairdresser's Weekly Journal*, 9 April 1910.

44 *Hairdresser's Weekly Journal*, 8 Jan 1910.

45 *Hairdresser's Weekly Journal*, 26 Feb 1910. Also 3 June 1882; 19 March, 9 April 1910.

46 *Hairdresser's Weekly Journal*, 30 Sep 1882.

47 *Hairdresser's Weekly Journal*, 19 March 1910.

48 Greenwood (1967), 41.

49 Greenwood (1967), 68. See too Rowntree and Kendall (1913), 49.

50 *Hairdresser's Weekly Journal*, 2 April 1910. Also 24 June 1882; 12 Feb, 12 March, 9 April 1910.

FINANCIAL SERVICES

1 Kent, M4, 30. Also G2, 111; Mrs M6B, 28; *Pawnbrokers' Gazette*, 25 Aug 1851; Reeves (1913), 72; Samuel (1981), 167.

2 *Sandbach Guardian*, 23 March 1895; *Pawnbrokers' Gazette*, 4 March 1850; *S C Betting*, 1902, Q. 2,009, J King; Mayhew (1861–2), I, 30; Manchester, M Dobkin, 8; Mrs Oulton, 2; Meacham (1977), 55; Roberts (1978), 106; White (1980), 59, 96.

3 Manchester, 811.

4 O'Mara (1934), 118. Information received from the Ocean Transport & Trading Limited, Liverpool.

5 Manchester, Mr Hardman, 2-3; also 791, 4; *Pawnbrokers' Gazette*, 4 March 1850; *Report by the Joint Select Committee . . . on the Moneylenders Bill*, 1924–5, Q. 722-3, 740-6, A Hunt.

6 *Report Moneylenders*, 1924–5, Q. 901, D C Keeling; *Pawnbrokers' Gazette*, 4 March 1850; Manchester, 797, 9; 811, 2; Lancaster, Mr G1P, 52; information from Elizabeth Roberts.

7 Manchester, 806, 2. Also 811, 2; *Report Moneylenders*, 1924–5, Q. 1,507, M Wilson.

8 Manchester, 788, 35; 806, 2; 811, 2; *Report from the Select Committee on Money Lending*, 1898, Q. 299, Judge Collier; *Report Moneylenders*, 1924–5, Q. 378, Colonel Watts-Morgan; Reeves (1913), 73; Paterson (1911), 47; Bowley and Hurst (1915), 137-8.

9 O'Mara (1934), 66. Also 68-9.

10 Manchester, 811, 1. Also 806, 2; *Report Moneylenders*, 1924–5, Q. 1,182, Sir F Blackwell; Rubin (1981).

11 O'Mara (1934), 67-8.

12 *Pawnbrokers' Gazette*, 10 Nov 1900; Manchester, 797, 9; Barnes (1976), 29-30, 42.

13 *Pawnbrokers' Gazette*, 10 Nov 1900.

14 Manchester, 795, 3.

15 Manchester, 791, 13. Also 539, 3-4; *Pawnbrokers' Gazette*, 4 Nov 1839; 15 July 1850.

16 *Pawnbrokers' Gazette*, 22 July 1839; 1 June, 13 July 1840; 14 Jan, 8 April 1850; 1 Sep 1851; 30 Jan 1860; *S C Public Houses*, 1852-3, Q. 6,375, Rev J Clay; *Report from the Select Committee on Pawnbrokers*, 1870, Q. 762, G Attenborough; Q. 1,028-9, J F May; Q. 2,067, A McKay.

17 *Pawnbrokers' Gazette*, 12 Oct 1840. Also 13 July, 28 Sep 1840; 19 Aug 1850; 'A Working Man' to *Scottish Times*, 10 March 1849.

18 *Pawnbrokers' Gazette*, 14 Jan, 11 March, 19 Aug, 9 Dec 1850; 3, 9 Jan 1860; *S C Pawnbrokers*, 1870, Q. 1,242-3, A M'Call; Q. 1,807, W Hector; Q. 2,061, A McKay; Q. 3,790, W M'Donald; Q. 4,395-8, 4,402, W Scoular.

19 *S C Pawnbrokers*, 1870, Q. 4,958, G Scotson; *Pawnbrokers' Gazette*, passim.

20 *Scottish Times*, 10 Feb 1849.

21 Manchester, 790, 10. Also 539, 8; *Pawnbrokers' Gazette*, 7 Jan, 4 Feb 1839; 4 Feb, 22 April 1850; 11 Aug 1900; *S C Pawnbrokers*, 1870, Q. 415, A Hardaker; Q. 2,063, A McKay; Q. 3,793, W M'Donald; Q. 4,404-5, W Scoular; *Report from the Select Committee on Pawnbrokers Bill*, 1872, Q. 21-2, G H Gilman.

22 *Pawnbrokers' Gazette*, 26 Oct 1840; 7 Jan 1850; 16 June 1851; 30 Jan 1860; *Scottish Times*, 10 Feb, 3 May 1849; *S C Pawnbrokers*, 1870, Q. 760, G Attenborough; Q. 2,064, A McKay; Q. 4,409, W Scoular; Q. 4,865, G Russell; *S C Pawnbrokers Bill*, 1872, Q. 257, G H Gilman.

23 *Wolverhampton Chronicle*, 24 Aug 1842; *Pawnbrokers' Gazette*, 25 March, 28 Oct 1839; 13 May, 29 July 1850; 14 April 1851; 13 Jan 1900; *Report from the Select Committee on Debtors (Imprisonment)*, 1909, Q. 2,431-2, E Bray; Babbington (1882), J. 409-10.

24 *Pawnbrokers' Gazette*, 15 Sep 1851. Also 25 Aug 1851; Manchester, 795, 1; *S C Pawnbrokers Bill*, 1872, Q. 56, G H Gilman.

25 *Pawnbrokers' Gazette*, 12 Oct 1840; 19 Aug, 9 Dec 1850; 1 Sep 1851; *S C Pawnbrokers*, 1870, Q. 2,065, A McKay; Q. 4,865, G Russell.

26 Josephs (1980), 42-3. Also Manchester, 539, 12.

RETAILING

1 Lancaster, Mr G2L, 7. For industrial theft, see Philips (1977), 181-2. For horse dealing, see Kent, K1 and for 'totting' see Kent, A1, 5; B3, 36; G5, 48-9; M4, 28; Lancaster, B3L, 11-12; Manchester, 699; Mayhew (1861–2), II, 146; III, 315; O'Mara (1934), 117-8; Samuel (1981), 224.

2 Common (1974), 3. See too Lancaster, B1L, 28; P1B, 19.

3 Briggs (1956), 13, 19; Alexander (1970), 3, 22; Shaw and Wild (1979), 279.

4 Kitchen (1940), 22. Also Kent, M4, 113; Lancaster, M1L, 54; P2L, 8; Babbington (1882), J. 354-6, 380; *Fish Trades Gazette*, 1 Sep 1883; Holman (1952), 88-9; Davis (1966), 129; Samuel (1975), 204, 209, 214.

5 Rowntree and Kendall (1913), 115.

6 Samuel (1977), 8-9.

7 Babbington (1882), J. 377. Also O'Mara (1934), 117-8; Philips (1977), 181-2.

8 Thomson and Smith (1877–8), 7, 58.

9 Folio (1858), 130; Booth (1892), I, 186, 203; Alexander (1970), 76.

10 Mayhew (1861–2), I, 177. Also *Wolverhampton Chronicle*, 24 July 1850; *Royal Commission on Liquor Licensing Laws, 3rd Report*, 1898, Q. 33,670, J Pearce.

11 *Hackney Carriage Guardian*, 28 Nov 1885.

12 Davies (1908), 187. Also Folio (1858), 27-8; Booth (1892), I, 58, 329; Mayhew (1861–2), I, 36; IV, 439; Kenney (1939), 23.

13 *Cab Trade Record*, May 1902. Also Folio (1858), vi; Babbington (1882), J. 441-2; *Labour Tribune* 3 May 1890; Manchester, J 42; Bennett (1914), 130; Williams (1976), 179; Lipman (1959), 59-60; White (1980), 245, 257.

14 Mayhew (1861–2), I, 105. Also Booth (1892), I, 58; Alexander (1970), 62.

15 Folio (1858), 138.

16 Mayhew (1861–2), I, 60. Also Blackman (1963), 96-7; Alexander (1970), 84-5, 233. Cf. Bienefeld (1975), 66-9.

17 Alexander (1970), 63-5. Also Shaw and Wild (1979), 280-1; Mayhew (1861–2), I, 5, 9. It is assumed of course that the efficiency of the census and the proportion of penny capitalists among street traders remained constant.

18 *Census*, 1851–1911. See also Malcolmson (1975), 46. Gerry Rubin informs me that these figures are consistent with the vitality of the credit trades as seen in county court records, 1871–1911.

19 Mayhew (1861–2), I, 4; II, 1; Briggs (1956), 115; Alexander (1970), 65, 68, 81, 84, 233; Ashby (1974), 201-2; Wild and Shaw (1975), 202; Horn (1976), 13.

20 Roberts (1973), 76. Also Essex County Record Office, D/DU 152/56, Case, 1834; Folio (1858), 15; Bear (1908), 42; *Report from the Joint Select Committee on Sunday Trading*, 1906, Q. 1,879, W Gentle; Foley (1973), 17; Storch (1976), 483, 498; information from Gerry Rubin.

21 Davies (1909), 114.
22 Mayhew (1861—2), I, 7, 9.
23 Booth (1892), I, 264. Also *Royal Commission on Market Rights and Tolls, 1st Report*, 1888, Q. 3,548, J Denton.
24 Mayhew (1861—2), I, 61.
25 Folio (1858), 26, 126-7, 129. Also Babbington (1882), J. 377; *Fish Trades Gazette*, 1 Sep 1883.
26 Booth (1892), I, 264. Also Alexander (1970), 77, 85; Kent, G2, 164.
27 Mayhew (1861—2), I, 105.
28 Bell (1907), 81.
29 Mayhew (1861—2), I, 324, 334. Folio (1858), 72-6; Davis (1966), 264; Alexander (1970), 78, 80.
30 Booth (1892), I, 67.
31 Tregenza (1977), 123.
32 Folio (1858), 108. Also 73-7, 89-90; Mayhew (1861—2), I, 326-7; Davies (1975), 138; Brown (1978), letter V.
33 Thomson and Smith (1877—8), 24.
34 Booth (1892), I, 58. Also Babbington (1882), J. 356, 379; *Fish Trades Gazette*, 1 Sep 1883; *R C Liquor Licensing, 3rd Report*, 1898, Q. 33,670, J Pearce; Folio (1858), 56; Davies (1908), 249; Hindley (1881), 28-9; Rees (1969), 4-7; Holford (1869), 3; Lancaster, Mr G1P, 54.
35 Henderson (1969), 99.
36 Kenney (1939), 89. Also Babbington (1882), J. 356.
37 'An Inhabitant' to *Wolverhampton Chronicle*, 17 July 1850. See too *Whitby Times*, 22 April 1870; *Fish Trades Gazette*, 16 June 1883.
38 Babbington (1882), J. 361, 434-5; *R C Market Rights, 1st Report*, 1888, Q. 5,836, J A Tolm; *Stockport Advertiser*, 4 Feb 1870; *Whitby Times*, 18 March 1870; *Fish Trades Gazette*, 9 June, 14 July 1883; 2 Feb 1901; *Hackney Carriage Guardian*, 7 Jan, 18 March, 27 May 1885.
39 Babbington (1882), J. 373, 377.
40 Treble (1978), 46.
41 Thomson and Smith (1877—8), 8.
42 Mayhew (1861—2), I, 57. Also 325-6.
43 Davies (1908), 196.
44 Mayhew (1861—2), I, 6, 54-5.
45 Thomson and Smith (1877—8), 8. Also Lipman (1959), 35; *S C Pawnbrokers Bill*, 1872, Q. 341, W Holford; Shaw (1948?), 26-7; Urwick (1904), 132; Greenwood (1967), 304.
46 Mayhew (1861—2), 9. Also Riverside Visitor (1892), 56-7; Greenwood (1967), 16; Anderson (1971), 24.
47 Samuel (1981), 55. Also 262, 290; *Small Trader*, 15 May 1915; *R C Market Rights, 1st Report*, 1888, Q. 5,848-72, J A Tolon; Samuel (1980).
48 Kent, B3, 25. Also Stedman Jones (1971), 227; Josephs (1980), 54.

49 *Hairdresser's Weekly Journal*, 16 Dec 1882. Also White (1980), 26, 122-3.

50 *S C Sale of Beer*, 1833, Q. 3,740, 3,753-5, J Bishop; Q. 4,060, T Cartwright; Q. 4,323, G Wells; *S C Public Houses*, 1852—3, Q. 1,328, T W W Brown; Q. 4,179, J Bishop; Lancaster, Mrs P2P, 19; Young (1979), 124.

51 Holman (1952), 90-91. Also Manchester, 584-5; *Scottish Times*, 11 Nov 1848; *R C Friendly Societies, 1st Report*, 1871, Q. 5,894, G Lea; Stacey and Wilson (1958), 33; Yamey (1954), 35; Alexander (1970), 236; Lambert (1975), 298; Longmate (1978), 100; Vigne and Howkins (1977), 187; Foley (1973), 19.

52 Coombes (1939), 21.

53 Vigne and Howkins (1977), 186-7.

54 *Fish Trades Gazette*, 22 Sep 1883. Also *Sandbach Guardian*, 2 Feb 1895; *S C Sale of Beer*, 1833, Q. 304, Rev J Haggett; Q. 535, T R Barker; Q. 855, J Parrott; Q. 1,617, S R Monte; Q. 3,302, W D Cooper; Q. 3,917-8, J Farren.

55 Kent, M4, 180.

56 Lancaster, M1L, 12. Also M3L, 13; H2B, 92; Manchester, 654.

57 Bell (1907), 70. Also *Pawnbrokers' Gazette*, 27 May 1850.

58 Roberts (1973), 82. Also *S C Sale of Beer*, 1833, Q. 2,371, P Townley; Q. 3,189, W D Cooper; Manchester, 480.

59 Mathias (1967), 50.

60 Nicholson (1975), 36.

61 Roberts (1973), 19.

62 Holman (1952), 49.

63 Vigne and Howkins (1977), 190.

64 Roberts (1973), 81-2.

65 *S C Sale of Beer*, 1833, Q. 3,326, W D Cooper. Also Q. 11, Rev R Wright; Q. 766, W Holmes; Q. 4,270, R Bryden; Q. 4,288, T Rowlandson; *S C Public Houses*, 1852—3, Q. 7,424, H Pownall; Kent, B10, 12; M7, 1-2; Lancaster, M5L, 18; Manchester, 884; *Whitby Times*, 25 March 1870.

66 *S C Sale of Beer*, 1833, Q. 3,958, J Lancaster. Also Q. 933, W Loraine; Q. 1,454, T C Bellington; Q. 4,313-4, G Wells; Q. 4,145-6, E Read.

67 *S C Sale of Beer*, 1833, Q. 4,098, 4,110, W Lowe; Q. 4,141-2, E Read; Q. 4,253, R Bryden; Q. 4,309, G. Wells; *Licensed Victuallers Gazette*, 24 Aug 1872; Roberts (1973), 4.

68 *S C Sale of Beer*, 1833, Q. 880, J Parrott; Q. 3,169-72, W D Cooper; *S C Public Houses*, 1852—3, Q. 6,859, G Hogg; *Licensed Victuallers Gazette*, 18 Jan, 22 March, 14 June 1873; Booth (1892), I, 34; Roberts (1977), 311.

69 *R C Liquor Licensing, 2nd Report*, 1897, Q. 15,424, 15,446, W McKenzie; *3rd Report*, 1898, Q. 29,739-40, L Carr; Q. 41,840-1, D Maclean; *5th Report*, 1898, Q. 44,024-51, D Dewar; Q. 45,422, T Wyness; Q. 48,571, D F Gordon; Q. 50,466-8, D Lewis; Q. 51,661, W Mackay; *Select Committee on Acts for the Regulation*

and Inspection of Mines, Q. 2,269, W Pickard; *Report from the Select Committee on the Club Registration Bill*, 1893—4, Q. 203-4, 212-13, A Llewhellin; Q. 1,742, F Beavan; Stephen (1896); *Western Mail*, 27 Feb 1871; 15 Nov 1913; Lambert (1972), 178; Lambert (1975), 298.

70 Roberts (1977), 31. See also Booth (1892), I, 59; Freeman (1914), 15-21, 29-40, 42-9, 55-7, 59-70.

71 *Wolverhampton Chronicle*, 31 July 1850. Also *S C Sale of Beer*, 1833, Q. 247, Rev R Wright; Q. 1,112-4, I Hughes; *S C Public Houses*, 1854, Q. 3,127-8, Sir J Paxton; Harrison (1971), 328-9.

72 Roberts (1973), 175. Also Lancaster, Mr M7B, 5, 33; W2B, 30-1; Kent, Mrs B18, 9; Mr D2, 25.

73 Lancaster, Mrs P2P, 20.

74 Mathias (1967), 41. Also *Small Trader*, 15 April 1915.

75 Lancaster, W1B, 25.

76 Reeves (1913), 97.

77 Roberts (1973), 102, 106. Also *R C Liquor Licensing, 5th Report*, 1898, Q. 51,383, J Dick.

78 Lancaster, Mrs P2P, 3, 6, 10. Also *Small Trader*, 15 March 1915; Payne (1974), 31, 34; Alexander (1970), 165.

79 Kent, Mrs B18, 8.

80 McGeown (1968), 31. Also Neild (1841), 322; Blackman (1967), 113.

81 Bundy and Healy (1978), 85.

82 Taylor (1903), 98-9.

83 Lancaster, Mr D2P, 43.

84 Storch (1976), 482-9; *R C Liquor Licensing, 3rd Report*, 1898, Q. 41,835, D Maclean; *Licensed Victuallers Gazette*, 17 May 1873; Williams (1978), 96.

85 Kent, B18, 5, 8. Also M7, 15; *S C Sale of Beer*, 1833, Q. 2,611, 2,632, J Hamer; Q. 3,209-10, W D Cooper; Lancaster, M2P, 132; Riverside Visitor (1892), 154.

86 Kent, M7, 28.

87 T Crabbe to *Hackney Carriage Guardian*, 24 April 1886; *Small Trader*, 15 Jan 1915; Jefferys (1954), 163; Mathias (1967), 4, 13-14; Foley (1973), 45; Crossick (1977), 24.

88 Longmate (1978), 101.

89 Roberts (1973), 19. See also *Small Trader*, 15 June 1915; Lancaster, M3B, 5; M7B, 3.

90 Davies (1909), 129.

91 *S C Sunday Trading*, 1906, Q. 2,377, J Sanders.

92 Booth (1892), I, 50. Also *S C Sale of Beer*, 1833, Q. 855, J Parrott; Q. 978, J Weyland; Q. 1,197, I Hughes; *R C Liquor Licensing, 3rd Report*, 1898, Q. 29,743-8, 30,000, L Carr; Lancaster, Mr G1P, 54-5; M1L, 28; Kent, S10, 130-1; Kitchen (1940), 22-3; Anderson (1971), 24; Foster (1974), 134, 136, 238.

93 Lancaster, M3B, 4-5.

94 Lancaster, Mrs P2P, 30. Also Klingender (1951), 16, 18.

95 Nicholson (1975), 13.
96 Crossick (1978), 114.

CONCLUSION

1   Lancaster; Roberts (1976); Roberts (1977).
2   Lancaster, Mr M6B, 48; Mr D2P, 27; Kent, B8, 66; Philips (1977),
    128, 180, 182; Humphries (1981), 24, 27.
3   Lancaster, Mr G1P, 26-8; Bundy and Healy (1978), 87; Humphries
    (1981), 25, 31; Samuel (1981), 9, 50.
4   Lancaster.
5   Bowley and Hurst (1915), 25; Davidoff (1979), 85; Samuel (1980).
6   Foster (1974), 229; Morris (1980), 15.
7   Lancaster; Freeman (1914), 15-21, 29-40, 42-9, 55-7, 59-74.
8   Roberts (1981), 8-10, 13-15. However Dr W M Walker informs me
    that he has found no such evidence of penny capitalism in the
    textile city of Dundee.
9   Crossick (1978), 47. Also 73; *S C Sale of Beer*, 1833, Q. 4,242,
    J Smith; *R C Liquor Licensing, 5th Report*, 1898, Q. 49,751, C
    Carlow; Boswell (1973), 45; Walton (1978), 54; Crossick (1979),
    21; Cannadine (1980), 409. Cf. Johnson (1981), 11.
10 Meacham (1977), 95; Williams (1978), 54; Benson (1980), 88-90;
    Hunt (1981), 3, 23.
11 Mayhew (1861–2), III, 224. Cf. Bienefeld (1975), 55-6.
12 *Sandbach Guardian*, 12 Jan 1895.
13 See for example, Bhalla (1973), 191; Firth (1946), 22-7; Taira
    (1966); Epstein (1968); Bienefeld (1975); Scott (1979) and
    Smith (1981).
14 Kent, G2, 164; information from Elizabeth Roberts. Cf. Mendels
    (1972), 242; McKendrick (1974); Malcolmson (1975), 40.
15 Cf. Bienefeld (1975), 64, 71-3; Malcolmson (1975), 28; Smith
    (1981), 45.
16 Roberts (1978), 50; Walton (1978), 86, 90; McKendrick (1974).
17 Kent, C17, 3.
18 Schmiechen (1975), 413.
19 *S C Labouring Poor*, 1843, *Report*, iv. See also Q. 997-9, F Pickard;
    Q. 2,061, Sir H Fletcher; Morris (1980).
20 See for example Kent, S10, 133; Morris (1979), 4; Goldthorpe
    (1980), 4-6.
21 Foster (1974), 326; Bechhofer *et. al.* (1974), 104.
22 Mayhew (1861–2), I, 20, 58; Anderson (1971), 24; Gray (1974),
    31; Foster (1974), 125 *et. seq.*, 238; Crossick (1977), 35; Crossick
    (1978); Vincent (1963–4), 76.
23 *The Tailor*, 3 Nov 1866.
24 Kay-Shuttleworth (1873), 71.
25 Chapman and Marquis (1912), 308, comment of Geoffrey Drage.
26 *R C on Labour, 2nd Report*, 1892, Q. 19,091, C Hobson.
27 Kent, T6, 10. Also Lancaster, Mr H6B, 99; Thompson (1974),
    385; Hobsbawm and Rudé (1973), 41; Benson (1980), 89; Barnsby
    (1980), 46-7.

28 Morris (1979), 55.
29 Checkland (1964), 221.
30 *S C Labouring Poor*, 1843, Q. 1,529, J Brooks. Also Q. 1,667-72, J Orange.

Bibliography

PRIMARY AUTHORITIES: MANUSCRIPT

Babbington, John, Autobiography, 1882 (British Library of Political and Economic Science).
Case between Pedlar and Shopkeepers, 1834 (Essex Record Office).

ORAL HISTORY COLLECTIONS

Manchester Studies, Manchester Polytechnic.
Roberts, Elizabeth, 'The Quality of Life in Two Lancashire Towns, 1880–1930' (University of Lancaster).
Roberts, Elizabeth, 'Social and Family Life in Preston, 1890–1940' (University of Lancaster).
Winstanley, Michael, 'Life in Kent before 1914' (University of Kent).

PRIMARY AUTHORITIES: PRINTED

Articles of Agreement made between the Members Of A Society, who have agreed to meet at the House of Mr. John Jones, . . ., Birmingham 1808 (Birmingham Reference Library).
Rules and Regulations of The Hope Iron Boat Club, Birmingham 1856 (Birmingham Reference Library).

OFFICIAL PUBLICATIONS

Census, 1801–1921.
Select Committee on Manufactures, Commerce, and Shipping, 1833.
Select Committee on the Sale of Beer, 1833.
Select Committee on Education of the Poorer Classes in England and Wales, 1838.
Select Committee on Labouring Poor (Allotments of Land), 1843.
Select Committee on Sunday Trading (Metropolis), 1847.
Select Committee on Public Houses, 1852–4.
Report of the Commissioners appointed to inquire into the State of Popular Education in England, 1861.
Select Committee on Acts for the Regulation and Inspection of Mines, 1866.

Select Committee on Pawnbrokers, 1870—1.
Royal Commission upon the Administration and Operation of the Contagious Diseases Acts, 1871.
Royal Commission on Friendly and Benefit Building Societies, 1871—4.
Select Committee on Pawnbrokers Bill, 1872.
Returns of the Number of Allotments detached from and attached to Cottages, 1886.
Royal Commission on Market Rights and Tolls, 1888.
Select Committee on Small Holdings, 1889.
Select Committee on Theatres and Places of Entertainment, 1892.
Royal Commission on Labour, 1892—4.
Select Committee on the Club Registration Bill, 1893—4.
Royal Commission on Liquor Licensing Laws, 1997—8.
Select Committee on Money Lending, 1898.
Select Committee of the House of Lords on Betting, 1901—2.
Joint Select Committee on Sunday Trading, 1906.
Select Committee on Debtors (Imprisonment), 1909.
Joint Select Committee . . . on the Moneylenders Bill, 1924—5.
Departmental Committee of Inquiry into Allotments, 1969.

NEWSPAPERS AND PERIODICALS

National
The Bioscope
Cab Trade Record
The Centaur
Colliery Guardian
The Era
Fishing News
Fish Trades Gazette
Hackney Carriage Guardian
The Hairdresser
Hairdresser's Weekly Journal
Labour Tribune
Licensed Victuallers Gazette
The Magnet
Pawnbrokers' Gazette
Photographic Work
Plumber and Decorator
Road Journal
Scottish Times
The Smallholder
The Tailor
The Waterman

Local
Aberdeen Journal
Bexhill-On-Sea Chronicle

Sandbach Guardian
Stockport Advertiser
Western Mail
Whitby Times
Wolverhampton Chronicle

AUTOBIOGRAPHIES AND BIOGRAPHIES

Anon, *Reminiscences of An Old Draper*, London 1876.

Ashby, M K, *Joseph Ashby Of Tysoe 1859–1919: A Study of English Village Life*, London 1974.

Barnes, Ron, *Coronation Cups And Jam Jars: A Portrait of an East End Family through Three Generations*, London 1976.

Brown, J D, *The Autobiography of a Beggar Boy*, London 1978.

Common, Jack, *Kiddar's Luck*, Glasgow 1974.

Coombes, B L, *These Poor Hands: The Autobiography of a Miner Working in South Wales*, London 1939.

Cooper, Thomas, *The Life of Thomas Cooper*, Leicester 1971.

Davies, W H, *The Autobiography of a Super-Tramp*, London 1924.

Davies, W H, *The Right Place, the Right Time: Memories of Boyhood Days in a Welsh Mining Community*, Swansea 1975.

Foley, Alice, *A Bolton Childhood*, Manchester 1973.

Goodman, J B ed., *Victorian Cabinet Maker: The Memoirs of James Hopkinson 1819–1894*, London 1968.

Greenwood, Walter, *There Was A Time*, London 1967.

Gresswell, Fred, *Bright Boots: An Autobiography and Anthology*, London 1956.

Hamilton, Peggy, *Three Years Or The Duration: The Memoirs of a Munition Worker, 1914–1918*, London 1978.

Hanson, William, *The Life of William Hanson, Written by Himself (in his 80th Year,) And Revised by a Friend*, Halifax 1884.

Harris, John, *My Autobiography*, London 1882.

Hindley, Charles ed., *The Life and Adventures of a Cheap Jack by One of the Fraternity*, London 1881.

Holman, Bob, *Behind the Diamond Panes: The Story of a Fife Mining Community*, Cowdenbeath 1952.

Kenney, R, *Westering: An Autobiography by Rowland Kenney*, London 1939.

Kitchen, Fred, *Brother to the Ox: The Autobiography of a Farm Labourer*, London 1940.

Langley, Tom, *The Tipton Slasher: His Life and Times*, Tipton n.d.

Lawson, Jack, *A Man's Life*, London 1944.

McGeown, Patrick, *Heat the Furnace Seven Times More*, London 1968.

Nicholson, Norman, *Wednesday Early Closing*, London 1975.

O'Mara, Pat, *The Autobiography of a Liverpool Irish Slummy*, London 1934.

Rider Haggard, L ed., *I Walked By Night: Being the Life & History of the King of the Norfolk Poachers Written by Himself*, Ipswich 1975.

Roberts, Robert, *The Classic Slum: Salford Life in the First Quarter of the Century*, Manchester 1971.

Samuel, Raphael, *East End Underworld: Chapters in the Life of Arthur Harding*, London 1981.

Shaw, Sam, *Guttersnipe*, London 1948(?).

Somerville, Alexander, *The Autobiography Of A Working Man*, London 1951.

Sturt, George, *A Small Boy In the Sixties*, Hassocks 1977.

Sturt, George, *A Memoir Of A Surrey Labourer*, Firle, Sussex 1978.

Taylor, Peter, *Autobiography of Peter Taylor*, Paisley 1903.

Tregenza, Leo, *Harbour Village: Yesterday in Cornwall*, London 1977.

Williams, Alfred, *Life in a Railway Factory*, Newton Abbot 1969.

OTHER AUTHORITIES LARGELY OR PARTLY PRIMARY IN NATURE

Ashby, A W, *Allotments and Small Holdings in Oxfordshire: A Survey made on behalf of the Institute for Research in Agricultural Economics, University of Oxford*, Oxford 1917.

Bayly, Mrs, *Ragged Homes, and How To Mend Them*, London 1860.

Bear, W E, 'Prospects for Small Holders', *Journal of the Bath and West and Southern Counties Society* (1908).

Bell, Lady, *At the Works: A Study of a Manufacturing Town*, London 1907.

Bennett, E N, *Problems of Village Life*, London 1914.

Booth, Charles, *Life And Labour Of The People in London*, London 1892.

Bowley, A L and Burnett-Hurst, A R, *Livelihood And Poverty: A study in the Economic Conditions of Working-Class Households in Northampton, Warrington, Stanley and Reading*, London 1915.

Chapman, S J and Marquis, F J, 'The Recruiting of the Employing Classes from the Ranks of the Wage-Earners in the Cotton Industry', *Journal of the Royal Statistical Society* lxxv/iii (Feb. 1912).

Davies, M F, *Life In An English Village: An Economic and Historical Survey of the Parish of Corsley in Wiltshire*, London 1909.

de Rousiers, Paul, *The Labour Question in Britain*, London 1896.

Folio, Felix, *The Hawkers and Street Dealers of Manchester, and the North of England Manufacturing Districts Generally . . .*, Manchester 1858.

Fortescue, Lord, 'Poor Men's Gardens', *The Nineteenth Century*, 23 (1888).

Freeman, Arnold, *Boy Life & Labour: The Manufacture of Inefficiency*, London 1914.

Frost, Thomas, *The Old Showmen and the Old London Fairs*, London 1874.

Green, J L, *Allotments and Small Holdings*, London 1896.

Holdenby, Christopher, *Folk Of The Furrow*, London 1913.

Holford, W, 'A Sketch of the Domestic Habits of the Families of a Poor District', *The London City Mission Magazine* (1 April 1869).

Hollingshead, John, *Ragged London In 1861*, London 1861.

Howarth, E G and Wilson, M, *West Ham: A Study in Social and Industrial Problems, being the Report of the Outer London Inquiry Committee*, London 1907.

Jebb, L, *The Small Holdings Of England: A Survey Of Various Existing Systems*, London 1907.

Kay-Shuttleworth, Sir James, *Thoughts and Suggestions on Certain Social Problems Contained Chiefly in Addresses to Meetings of Workmen in Lancashire*, London 1873.

Levy, Hermann, *Large and Small Holdings: A Study of English Agricultural Economics*, Cambridge 1911.

Loane, M, *From Their Point of View*, London 1908.

M'Iver, Daniel, *An Old-time Fishing Town: Eyemouth its History, Romance, and Tragedy, with an Account of The East Coast Disaster, 14th October, 1881*, Greenock 1906.

Mayhew, Henry, *London Labour and the London Poor*, London 1861-2.

Meyer, C and Black, C, *Makers Of Our Clothes: A Case for Trade Boards*, London 1909.

Neild, William, 'Comparative Statement of the Income and Expenditure of Certain Families of the Working Classes in Manchester and Dukinfield, in the Years 1836 and 1841', *Journal of the Statistical Society of London* iv (1841).

Paterson, Alexander, *Across The Bridges or Life by the South London River-Side*, London 1911.

Read, C S, 'Large and Small Holdings: a Comparative View', *Journal of the Royal Agricultural Society* xxiii/i (1887).

Reeves, M P, *Round About A Pound A Week*, London 1913.

"Riverside Visitor", *The Pinch Of Poverty: Sufferings and Heroism of the London Poor*, London 1892.

Rowntree, B S, *Poverty: A Study of Town Life*, London 1902.

Rowntree, B S, *Betting & Gambling: A National Evil*, London 1905.

Rowntree, B S and Kendall, M, *How The Labourer Lives: A Study of the Rural Labour Problem*, London 1913.

Stephen, H L, 'Sunday Closing in Operation', *Fortnightly Review* (Aug 1896).

Stirton, Thomas, 'Small Holdings', *Journal of the Royal Agricultural Society* v (1894).

Thomson, J and Smith, A, *Street Life In London*, London 1877—8.

Udale, James, 'Market Gardening and Fruit Growing in the Vale of Evesham', *Journal of the Royal Agricultural Society* lxix (1908).

Urwick, E J ed., *Studies of Boy Life in our Cities*, London 1904.

Webb, Sidney and Beatrice, *Industrial Democracy*, London 1913.

SECONDARY AUTHORITIES: BOOKS AND PAMPHLETS

Alexander, David, *Retailing in England during the Industrial Revolution*, London 1970.

Allen, G C, *British Industries And Their Organization*, London 1959.

Anderson, Michael, *Family Structure in Nineteenth Century Lancashire*, Cambridge 1971.

Barnsby, G V, *Social Conditions in the Black Country 1800–1900*, Wolverhampton 1980.

Benson, John, *British Coalminers in the Nineteenth Century: A Social History*, Dublin 1980.

Boswell, Jonathan, *The Rise and Decline of Small Firms*, London 1973.

Bowley, Marian, *The British Building Industry: Four Studies in Response and Resistance to Change*, Cambridge 1966.

Briggs, Asa, *Friends of the People: the Centenary History of Lewis's*, London 1956.

Burgess, K, *The Origins of British Industrial Relations: The Nineteenth Century Experience*, London 1975.

Bythell, Duncan, *The Sweated Trades: Outwork in Nineteenth-century Britain*, London 1978.

Calvert, Albert F, *Salt In Cheshire*, London 1915.

Cannadine, David, *Lords and Landlords: the Aristocracy and the Towns 1774–1967*, Leicester 1980.

Chambers, J D and Mingay, G E, *The Agricultural Revolution 1750–1880*, London 1966.

Chanan, Michael, *The Dream that Kicks: The Prehistory and Early Years of Cinema in Britain*, London 1980.

Checkland, S G, *The Rise of Industrial Society in England 1815–1885*, London 1964.

Common, Jack ed., *Seven Shifts*, London 1938.

Crossick, Geoffrey ed., *The Lower Middle Class in Britain 1870–1914*, London 1977.

Crossick, Geoffrey, *An Artisan Elite in Victorian Society: Kentish London 1840–1880*, London 1978.

Cunningham, Hugh, *Leisure in the Industrial Revolution, c.1780–c.1880*, London 1980.

Davies, J A, *Education in a Welsh Rural County 1870–1973*, Cardiff 1973.

Davis, Dorothy, *A History Of Shopping*, London 1966.

Epstein, T S, *Capitalism Primitive and Modern: Some Aspects of Tolai Economic Growth*, Manchester 1968.

Finnegan, Frances, *Poverty and Prostitution: a Study of Victorian Prostitutes in York*, Cambridge 1979.

Firth, Raymond, *Malay Fishermen: Their Peasant Economy*, London 1946.

Forman, Charles, *Industrial Town: Self Portrait of St Helens in the 1920s*, St Albans 1979.

Foster, John, *Class Struggle and the Industrial Revolution: Early Industrial Capitalism in Three English Towns*, London 1974.

Goldthorpe, J H, *Social Mobility and Class Structure in Modern Britain*, Oxford 1980.

Griffiths, Neil, *Shops Book: Brighton 1900–1930*, Brighton 1978 or 79.

Hall, P G, *The Industries Of London Since 1861*, London 1962.

Hanson, Harry, *The Canal Boatmen 1760–1914*, Manchester 1975.

Harrison, Royden ed., *Independent Collier: The Coal Miner as Archetypal Proletarian Reconsidered*, Hassocks 1978.

Hartley, Marie and Ingilby, Joan, *The Old Hand-Knitters of The Dales*, Clapham via Lancaster 1969.

Henderson, W O, *The Lancashire Cotton Famine 1861–1865*, Manchester 1969.

Hobsbawm, E J and Rudé, G, *Captain Swing*, Harmondsworth 1973.

Horn, Pamela, *Labouring Life in the Victorian Countryside*, Dublin 1976.

Horn, Pamela, *Education in Rural England 1800–1914*, Dublin 1978.

Howarth, Ken, *Dark Days: Memories of the Lancashire & Cheshire Coalmining Industry*, Manchester 1978.

Howell, Michael and Ford, Peter, *The True History of the Elephant Man*, Harmondsworth 1980.

Hunt, E I, *British Labour History 1815–1914*, London 1981.

Jefferys, J B, *Retail Trading In Britain 1850–1950: A Study of Trends in Retailing with Special Reference to the Development of Co-operative, Multiple Shop and Department Store Methods of Trading*, Cambridge 1954.

Jones, E L, *The Development of English Agriculture 1815–1873*, London 1968.

Josephs, Zoe, *Birmingham Jewry 1749–1914*, Birmingham 1980.

Klingender, F D, *The Little Shop*, London 1951.

Leather, John, *The Northseamen: The Story of the Fishermen, Yachtsmen and Shipbuilders of the Colne and Blackwater Rivers*, Lavenham 1971.

Lipman, V D, *A Century of Social Service 1859–1959: The Jewish Board of Guardians*, London 1959.

Longmate, Norman, *The Hungry Mills: The Story of the Lancashire Cotton Famine 1861–5*, London 1978.

McCann, P ed., *Popular Education and Socialization in the Nineteenth Century*, London 1977.

McHugh, Paul, *Prostitution and Victorian Social Reform*, London 1980.

Malcolmson, R W, *Popular Recreations in English Society 1700–1850*, Cambridge 1973.

Marsh, E J, *Sailing Drifters: The Story of the Herring Luggars of England, Scotland and the Isle of Man*, London c.1952.

Mathias, Peter, *Retailing Revolution: A History of Multiple Retailing in the Food Trades based upon the Allied Suppliers Group of Companies*, London 1967.

Meacham, Standish, *A Life Apart: The English Working Class 1890–1914*, London 1977.

Mills, Dennis R, *Lord and Peasant in Nineteenth Century Britain*, London 1980.

Mingay, G E, *Enclosure and the Small Farmer in the Age of the Industrial Revolution*, London 1968.

More, Charles, *Skill and the English Working Class, 1870–1914*, London 1980.

Morris, R J, *Class and Class Consciousness in the Industrial Revolution 1780–1850*, London 1979.

Norfolk Federation of Women's Institutes, *Within Living Memory: A Collection of Norfolk Reminiscences*, Norwich 1972.

Ord-Hume, A W J G, *Barrel Organ: The Story of the Mechanical Organ and its Repair*, London 1978.

Orwin, C S and Wheltham, E H, *History of British Agriculture 1846–1914*, London 1964.

Payne, P L, *British Entrepreneurship in the Nineteenth Century*, London 1974.

Philips, David, *Crime and Authority in Victorian England: The Black Country*, London 1977.

Price, Richard, *Masters, Unions and Men: Work Control in Building and the Rise of Labour*, Cambridge 1980.

Raistrick, A and Jennings, B, *A History of Lead Mining in the Pennines*, London 1965.

Rees, Goronwy, *St Michael: A History of Marks and Spencer*, London 1969.

Robin, Jean, *Elmdon: Continuity and Change in a North-west Essex Village 1861–1964*, Cambridge 1980.

Samuel, Raphael ed., *Village Life And Labour*, London 1975.

Samuel, Raphael ed., *Miners, Quarrymen and Saltworkers*, London 1977.

Stacey, N A H and Wilson, A, *The Changing Pattern of Distribution*, London 1958.

Starsmore, Ian, *English Fairs*, London 1975.

Stedman Jones, G, *Outcast London: A Study in the Relationship between Classes in Victorian Society*, Oxford 1971.

Sturt, Mary, *The Education of the People: A History of Primary Education in England and Wales in the Nineteenth Century*, London 1967.

Tax, Sol, *Penny Capitalism: A Guatemalan Indian Economy*, Washington 1953.

Thompson, Paul, *The Edwardians: The Remaking of British Society*, St Albans 1977.

Tunstall, Jeremy, *The Fishermen*, London 1962.

Walton, J K, *The Blackpool Landlady: A Social History*, Manchester 1978.

Wardle, David, *Education and Society in Nineteenth-Century Nottingham*, Cambridge, 1971.

West, E G, *Education and the Industrial Revolution*, London 1975.

Whitbread, Nanette, *The Evolution of the Nursery-Infant School: A History of Infant and Nursery Education in Britain, 1800–1970*, London 1972.

White, Jerry, *Rothschild Buildings: Life in an East End Tenement Block 1887–1920*, London 1980.

Willan, T S, *River Navigation in England 1600–1750*, London 1964.
Williams, Bill, *The Making of Manchester Jewry 1740–1875*, Manchester 1976.
Williams, Gwyn A, *The Merthyr Rising*, London 1978.
Williams, J E, *The Derbyshire Miners: A Study in Industrial and Social History*, London 1962.
Wilson, Robert J, *The Number Ones: The Story of the Life of Owner Boatmen on the Midland Canals*, Kettering 1973.
Winstanley, Michael J, *Life In Kent At the Turn of the Century*, Folkestone 1978.
Young, J D, *The Rousing of the Scottish Working Class*, London 1979.

ARTICLES

Bechhofer, F, Elliott, B, Rushforth, M and Bland, R. 'The Petits Bourgeois in the Class Structure: The Case of the Small Shopkeepers', *The Social Analysis of Class Structure*, ed. Frank Parkin, London 1974.
Bhalla, A S, 'Self-Employment in Less Developed Countries: Some Aspects of Theory and Policy', *Employment Creation in Developing Societies: The Situation of Labour in Dependent Economies*, ed. Karl Wohlmuth, New York 1973.
Bienefeld, M, 'The Informal Sector and Peripheral Capitalism: The Case of Tanzania', *Institute of Development Studies Bulletin* 6/3 (Feb 1975).
Blackman, J, 'The Food Supply of an Industrial Town: A Study of Sheffield's Public Markets 1780–1900', *Business History* v/2 (1963).
Blackman, J, 'The Development of the Retail Grocery Trade in the Nineteenth Century', *Business History* ix/2 (1967).
Bundy, Colin and Healy, Dermot, 'Aspects of Urban Poverty', *Oral History* 6/1 (Spring 1978).
Carpenter, Edward, 'Kettlenet Fishing', *Kent Life* (May 1975).
Chartres, J A, 'Road Carrying in England in the Seventeenth Century: Myth and Reality', *Economic History Review* xxx/1 (1977).
Colls, Robert, ' "Oh Happy English Children": Coal, Class and Education in the North-East', *Past and Present* 73 (Nov 1976).
Constantine, S, 'Amateur Gardening and Popular Recreation in the 19th and 20th Centuries', *Journal of Social History* xiv (Spring 1981).
Crossick, Geoffrey, 'La petite bourgeoisie britannique au XIXe siecle', *le mouvement social* 108 (1979).
Davidoff, L, 'The Separation of Home and Work? Landladies and Lodgers in Nineteenth- and Twentieth-Century England', *Fit Work for Women*, ed. S Burman, London 1979.
Davies, A C, 'The Old Poor Law in an Industrializing Parish: Aberdare, 1818–36', *Welsh History Review* viii/3 (1977).
Devine, T M, 'The Rise and Fall of Illicit Whisky-making in Northern Scotland, c. 1780–1840', *Scottish Historical Review*, liv (1975).

Dyos, H J, 'The Speculative Builders and Developers of Victorian London', *Victorian Studies* xi (1968).

Editorial Collective, 'British Economic History and the Question of Work', *History Workshop* 3 (Spring 1977).

Everitt, A, 'Town and Country in Victorian Leicestershire: The Role of the Village Carrier', *Perspectives in English Urban History*, ed. A Everitt, London 1973.

Fairburn, R A, 'An Account of a Small Nineteenth-Century Lead Mining Company on Alston Moor', *Industrial Archaeology Review* iv/3 (Autumn 1980).

Gatrell, V A C, 'Labour, Power, and the Size of Firms in Lancashire Cotton in the Second Quarter of the Nineteenth Century', *Economic History Review* xxx/1 (1977).

Glen, I A, 'A Maker of Illicit Stills', *Scottish Studies* 14/1 (1970).

Gray, R Q, 'The Labour Aristocracy in the Victorian Class Structure', *The Social Analysis of Class Structure*, ed. Frank Parkin, London 1974.

Hartwell, R M, 'The Service Revolution: The Growth of Services in Modern Economy', *The Fontana Economic History of Europe: The Industrial Revolution*, Glasgow 1973.

Higginson, J H, 'Dame Schools', *British Journal of Educational Studies* xxii/2 (June 1974).

Humphries, Stephen, 'Steal to Survive: The Social Crime of Working Class Children 1890–1940', *Oral History Journal* 9/1 (Spring 1981).

Johnson, P, 'Unemployment and Self-employment: a Survey', *Industrial Relations Journal* 12/5 (Sep-Oct 1981).

Lambert, W R, 'The Welsh Sunday Closing Act, 1881', *Welsh History Review* vi/2 (1972).

Lambert, W R, 'Drink and Work Discipline in Industrial South Wales, c.1800–1870', *Welsh History Review* vii/3 (1975).

Leinster-MacKay, D P, 'Dame Schools: A Need for Review', *British Journal of Educational Studies* xxiv/1 (Feb 1976).

McKendrick, N, 'Home Demand and Economic Growth: A New View of the Role of Women and Children in the Industrial Revolution', *Historical Perspectives: Studies in English Thought and Society*, ed. N McKendrick, London 1974.

McKibbin, Ross, 'Working-Class Gambling in Britain 1880–1939', *Past and Present* 82 (Feb 1979).

Malcolmson, P E, 'Getting a Living in the Slums of Victorian Kensington', *The London Journal* 1/1 (May 1975).

Marglin, Stephen A, 'What Do Bosses Do? The Origins and Functions of Hierarchy in Capitalist Production', *Review of Radical Political Economy* 6/2 (Summer 1974).

Markovitch, Tihomir J, 'The Dominant Sectors of French Industry', *Essays In French Economic History*, ed. Rondo Cameron, Homewood, Illinois 1970.

Mendels, Franklin F, 'Proto-industrialization: The First Phase of the Industrialization Process', *Journal of Economic History* xxxii/1 (March 1972).

Morris, R J, 'Whatever Happened to the British Working Class, 1750–1850?', *Bulletin of the Society for the Study of Labour History* 41 (Autumn 1980).

Richards, Eric, 'Women in the British Economy since about 1700: An Interpretation', *History* 59/197 (Oct 1974).

Roberts, Elizabeth, 'Working-Class Standards of Living in Barrow and Lancaster, 1890–1914', *Economic History Review* xxx/2 (1977).

Rule, John, 'The British Fisherman 1840–1914', *Bulletin of the Society for the Study of Labour History* 27 (Autumn 1973).

Rule, John, 'The Home Market and Sea Fisheries of Devon and Cornwall in the Nineteenth Century', *Population and Marketing: Two Studies in the History of the South-West*, ed. W Minchinton, Exeter 1976.

Samuel, Raphael, 'Industrial Crime in the 19th Century', *Bulletin of the Society for the Study of Labour History* 25 (Autumn 1972).

Samuel, Raphael, 'Workshop of the World: Steam Power and Hand Technology in mid-Victorian Britain', *History Workshop* 3 (Spring 1977).

Schmiechen, J A, 'State Reform and the Local Economy: an Aspect of Industrialization in Late Victorian and Edwardian London', *Economic History Review* xxviii/3 (1975).

Scott, A M, 'Who are the Self-Employed?', *Casual Work and Poverty in Third World Cities*, ed. R Bromley and C Gerry, Chichester 1979.

Shaw, G and Wild, M T, 'Retail Patterns in the Victorian City', *Transactions of the Institute of British Geographers* 1979.

Smith, Adrian, 'The Informal Economy', *Lloyds Bank Review* 141 (July 1981).

Storch, R S, 'The Policeman as Domestic Missionary: Urban Discipline and Popular Culture in Northern England, 1850–1880', *Journal of Social History* ix (1976).

Taira, Koji, 'The Relation Between Wages and Income from Self-Employment: Estimates and International Comparisons', *Manchester School of Economic and Social Studies* 34 (1966).

Thompson, E P, 'Patrician Society, Plebeian Culture', *Journal of Social History* vii (1974).

Thompson, F M L, 'Nineteenth-Century Horse Sense', *Economic History Review* xxix/1 (1976).

Thompson, F M L, 'Social Control in Victorian Britain', *Economic History Review* xxxiv/2 (1981).

Thorpe, H, 'The Homely Allotment: From Rural Dole To Urban Amenity: A Neglected Aspect of Urban Land Use', *Geography* 60/3 (July 1975).

Treble, J H, 'The Seasonal Demand for Adult Labour in Glasgow, 1890–1914', *Social History* 3/1 (1978).

Vigne, T and Howkins, A, 'The Small Shopkeeper in Industrial and Market Towns', *The Lower Middle Class in Britain*, ed. Geoffrey Crossick, London 1977.

Vincent, J R, 'The Electoral Sociology of Rochdale', *Economic History Review*, xvi/1 (1963–4).

Walkowitz, Judith, 'The Making of an Outcast Group: Prostitutes and Working Women in Nineteenth-Century Plymouth and Southampton', *A Widening Sphere: Changing Roles of Victorian Women*, ed. M Vicinus, Bloomington, Indiana 1977.

Walton, J K and McGloin, P R, 'The Tourist Trade in Victorian Lakeland', *Northern History* xvii (1981).

Wild, M T and Shaw, G, 'Population Distribution and Retail Provision: The Case of the Halifax-Calder Valley Area of West Yorkshire During the Second Half of the Nineteenth Century', *Journal of Historical Geography* 1/2 (1975).

Williams, Bill, 'The Jewish Immigrant In Manchester: The Contribution of Oral History', *Oral History* 7/1 (Spring 1979).

Wilson, Charles, 'The Entrepreneur in the Industrial Revolution', *History* 42/145 (June 1957).

Yamey, Basil, 'The Evolution of Shopkeeping', *Lloyds Bank Review* (Jan 1954).

UNPUBLISHED PAPERS AND THESES

Behagg, Clive, 'The Changing Role and Nature of Small Producers in the First Half of the Nineteenth Century',(Paper read at Social History Seminar, Birmingham University, 1980).

Douglas, Gavin, 'Yachting On The Colne: Some Preliminary Observations', (Essex University oral history project 9, n.d.).

Grant, E J, 'The Spatial Development of the Warwickshire Coalfield', (Birmingham University Ph D thesis, 1977).

Grass, John, 'Morecambe: The People's Pleasure: The Development of a Holiday Resort, 1880–1902', (Lancaster University M A thesis, 1972).

Hostettler, Eve, 'Cottage Economy 1900: an Exploration into the Conditions of Domestic Life amongst the Rural Labouring Class circa 1890–1910, Based on Oral Evidence', (Essex University oral history project 5, 1976).

Miller, Robin, 'Gambling and the British Working Class 1870–1914', (Edinburgh University M A dissertation, 1974).

Roberts, E A M, 'The Working-Class Family In Barrow And Lancaster', (Lancaster University Ph D thesis, 1978).

Roberts, Elizabeth, 'Working-Class Standards of Living in Three Lancashire Towns, 1890–1914', (Unpublished paper, 1981).

Rubin, G R, 'Bagmen, Packmen and "Perambulating Scotchmen": The Tally Trade and the County Courts in Nineteenth and Early Twentieth Century England', (Unpublished paper, 1981).

Samuel, Raphael, 'Back Street Trades in Bethnal Green', (Paper read at Social History Society conference, Winchester, 1981).

Seeley, J Y E, 'Coal Mining Villages of Northumberland and Durham: A Study of Sanitary Conditions and Social Facilities, 1870–1880', (Newcastle University M A thesis, 1973).

Index

170